God's Stubborn Girl
Cross-Cultural Evidence of Grace
by Margaret Fisher

"Has anyone ever called you stubborn?" The young woman stopped me in the hallway and caught me completely off guard. I was at a conference, when my family's life was about to be radically changed. We were heading to South Asia. We were going to try to start a business there and share our hope with our neighbors. We had gone through training, we were packing our bags, and we were saying our goodbyes. Then, this lady had the gall to step right into my reality.

"Well, yeah, all the time!" I couldn't help responding, automatically. It tended to be a trademark. It was a family trait, but I had more of it than most people told me was healthy. Sometimes, I felt ashamed that I was so slow to back down, but I was too stubborn to change.

"What some people call stubbornness, God is going to use as perseverance. It's His gift to you." She smiled at me, I offered her a hug, thanked her, and she went on her way. I stood there, still rocking my fussy baby back and forth on my hip. If you had asked me then, I would have told you that I didn't particularly want the gift of perseverance. If I were going to have to utilize perseverance, it would mean that there was something that I needed to persevere through. That didn't sound fun at all. That didn't sound like the international adventure I had hoped we were signing up for. That sounded like hard work. That sounded like disappointment. That sounded like heartache. Our time to get on the plane was looming and these were the comforting words that God spoke to me through a complete stranger.

The thing was, they were the exact words I needed to hear. I didn't need to hear another story about an international worker who beat all odds and saw amazing change come. I didn't need another story of a woman who had all the answers and found things were easier than she'd thought. This wasn't going to be my reality. I needed to hear that God's plan is sometimes perseverance — to just keep moving. I needed to hear that it was okay to be stubborn when it came to my life in Asia. I needed to know that there was a place for continuing on when you didn't see the fruit of all that you were doing — putting one determined foot in front of another.

I also needed to hear that it was God's gift to me. I could start to think that perseverance was my own doing. In the first five years in Asia, I was beaten too many times to think that any of the strength I had came from me. Perseverance was God's gracious gift to me. Perseverance was His strength in my weakness. Perseverance was my desperate whisper, "Lord, to whom shall I go? You have the words of eternal life." Perseverance was my battle cry, "If God is for me, who can be against me?" Perseverance was my confession, "Though He slay me, yet will I trust in him."

So, here is a story before any big success. Here is a story before any visible fruit. Here is a story of God's Stubborn Girl.

Big City

1

There was a day when we said goodbye. It was time to go. We had completed all the training. We had the prayer partners all signed up. We formatted a newsletter. We packed and repacked and repacked our six suitcases and four carry-ons. We went to all the goodbye parties and goodbye lunches. We had everything set up for our departure. We had contacted the ones who would receive us on arrival. We cried a lot. We were excited. We were prayed over and prayed over and prayed over. It was time to go.

I'm not sure anyone could prepare you for those goodbye hugs. The realization that you won't see these people for a long time — maybe forever. As we prepared to get on the plane, I hugged my Dad one last time. He was sick. He had stage four lung cancer. A miracle was the only hope for his recovery. We had discovered his illness about eight months before. There were plenty of sympathetic voices. There were voices who asked if we would like more time. There were voices that pressed guilt into us, telling us we should really stay on account of my Dad, on account of our kids being so small, on account of my pregnancy (I was four and a half months pregnant). My Dad's voice said, "Don't you dare stay here on account of me. You get on that plane." Gosh, I love him.

So, we hugged our families one last time. Bill strapped himself down with all of our luggage until you could hardly see him through the bulk. I took three-year-old Carl by the hand and cinched one and a half-year-old James tighter to my hip in the sling and we walked into the airport. We were flying on an Asian airline straight from Chicago to the Big City, so we thought. Fourteen hours in a plane. Three seats for four and a half people. As soon as we got in line, we started to leave America and arrived in South Asia. Almost all our fellow travelers were South Asians or of South Asian descent. Almost all the flight staff were South Asian. We reached the line, and were immediately asked to put our carry-on luggage on the scale. It turned out the regulation for carry-ons had changed since the day I checked the weight limit. We were over on almost every bag. Of course we were. We were trying to pack for two years of life in a new country in what we could bring on the plane for free. So, the immaculate packing and duct-taping and tie-wrapping we had accomplished was quickly mutilated as we desperately tried to reorganize right there in line. And we weren't the only ones.

There were at least ten families around us who were frantically throwing not-so-needed items to their relatives who dropped them off as they, also, tried to meet the new weight limit. The first moment of culture shock.

After that, we entered the impossibly long line and watched the minutes tick away. We started getting nervous that we wouldn't make our plane. Carl started fussing from standing there so long and getting pinched by every lady and man in line who thought he was cute. Which was about everybody. That might have been when Bill first started practicing our Carl-has-had-enough technique. He'd put Carl up on his shoulders. Carl could see what was going on while being out of reach of the admirers. Carl spent most of our first year in the country on Bill's shoulders.

As we got on the plane, we were reminded that we were no longer in America. People were pushing to get the best seats, pretending they hadn't realized that their ticket was, in fact, the middle seat and not the window seat they had plopped down in. People were maneuvering and re-negotiating because the airline hadn't ensured that their families would be sitting together. People were standing smack-dead in the aisle rearranging and rearranging their bags in the overhead bins while the line behind them piled up. People were ringing their attendant buttons and asking for drinks before the plane had moved away from the gate. I realized I was going to have a lot of things to get used to.

Our seats were, thankfully, together. Bill sat on one side of Carl and I sat on the other side with James on my lap, strategically straddling my large belly. Since this was my third baby, even though I was only four and a half months pregnant, I looked like many women do when they're seven months pregnant. In fact, we were questioned several times as we traveled just how far along I was. I think they wanted to make sure I had permission to fly. I can understand. No flight attendant wants to deliver a baby in the middle of a fourteen hour flight.

As we started off, there was a vague announcement from the cockpit that we would be landing in Frankfurt to refuel. What? I thought we were just getting this done! No, we had to land for a few hours and weren't allowed to exit the plane. So, our fourteen hour flight turned very quickly into a sixteen hour one. Just what we were hoping for! The boys really didn't do too shabby on the plane. Carl loved that he was allowed to watch as many movies as he wanted. James wasn't entertained by the movies all that much, but I could usually get him to fall asleep if I walked him back and forth around the cabin a few times. Then I'd have a few hours' relaxation before he woke up again. We had just gotten Carl to turn the TV off and take a rest when we touched down in Frankfurt. Well, that didn't last long. They had to turn everything off, so there were no movies and no escape for the next two hours. That was the hardest part of the journey. The boys fidgeted, whined, screamed, and grumped as we silently prayed for the flight crew to hurry up, already! Finally, they got the plane moving again and we managed to get the boys back to sleep. Bill, our family's champion sleeper, got some shut-eye during that flight, but between jostling boys, my baby belly, and my restless legs, I slept none. At one time, I remember having both boys laying on me and needing to go to the bathroom SO BAD! I just sat there and sat there because they were sleeping. I almost went berserk.

We landed in the evening. As soon as we landed, we headed for the bathrooms and then to get our luggage. Our friend was supposed to meet us there and bring us to the flat we'd be leasing for the first two months. All I remember about that drive was how crowded things were, how dirty, how HOT and HUMID, and how the driving situation reminded me of South America. But crazier.

I just kept looking around at all the people, trying to take it all in. Even at 8:00 at night, the roads were very busy and every inch of space was filled with people. There were people sleeping on the ground beneath the overpasses. There were people playing soccer on the grass between the curves of the roads. There were two to five people crammed on a motorcycle or in the back of a rickshaw. There were pedestrians, rickshaws, auto-rickshaws, bullock carts, cars, taxis, busses, cows, dogs, men pushing peddler carts, women carrying things on their heads, children knocking on the windows asking for change. I was just struck by the sheer number of people crammed into this small space. Coming from an area where there were usually less than twenty people per square mile, having more than 65,000 people per square mile was pretty overwhelming.

We wound our way through the traffic in the non-AC cab from the airport. It was a tiny van, but we crammed six of us plus all our luggage into it. We ended up in front of a fairly new-looking apartment complex. Our bags were unloaded and we lugged them and our now-sleeping kids down the hall to our new home for . . . one night. Oh, did I mention, the next day we were flying out for some meetings in Thailand? Yep.

The door to the apartment opened, a blessed rush of AC washed over us, and smiles greeted us. The couple that lived there was about to leave, but we were going to share the house for this night. We were introduced, met their two girls (about six months younger than our boys), and shoved our things into a room. There was food waiting for us and a few other new neighbors dropped in to say hello. Even though we were exhausted from the travel, James and Carl woke up with the prospect of playing with the new friends and we woke up with the rush of cool air and comfortable seats and good food. It was great to see welcoming faces, hear English, and know that this fairly large, nicely furnished, AC-containing home was to be ours for the next few months.

As we sat and chatted, though, the weariness of those long, tense miles washed over me. I had probably not slept for forty hours. I started to wonder if I shouldn't find a place to rest soon. All of a sudden, I heard a scream and then crying. Uh oh. I rushed to where the kids were playing and found, to my horror, that James had bitten the older daughter of our wonderful hosts. Aaaaggghhh! Of course, they were more than understanding, but I felt miserable. There we were, ready to make a difference in a new country, barely off the plane, and I could see the bite marks on that sweet girl's shoulder. Well, thus began my lesson in not being the world's perfect family. Many times we think that in order to make a difference, we have to have everything in order. Now, as I look back on that confused, ashamed, exhausted, pregnant, clueless mother, I know that I had NOTHING in order. People ask us, "Would you recommend people to go to a new country the way you did?" And I respond emphatically, "NO! It was ridiculous. Sheer folly. Difficult beyond what I could explain." And then I respond, "But, if it is how God calls them, they will make it. If God is in the middle of it, then they will survive." According to statistics and common sense, we did everything wrong. We came to the wrong place, at the wrong time of year, at the wrong season in life, with emotional baggage at home. It doesn't make sense and never could. But, God's wisdom and His will don't need to make sense for them to be correct. As I lay me down to sleep that night, I really don't think anything was running through my head except, 'Sleep, blessed sleep!' I had no idea what God had planned for the next phase in my journey. It was probably better that way. God gave us the blessed gift of ignorance.

Even before my body could fully unwind, I heard a soon-to-be familiar cry: "Mama, I'm hungry!" James. I'd probably slept two hours and he was up. From that point on, either one of the boys or both were awake until morning. Jet lag is a beast. Jet lag with young kids is a furious, fire-breathing leviathan. Thus began our two weeks of sleepless nights and weary days. Bill and I took turns trying to keep the kids occupied while the other one slept, but there were never enough hours in the day -- excuse me, night — to catch up with what we'd lost.

After that first journey, we had to muster our courage, rearrange our luggage, and head back to the airport that morning. We were going to Thailand. We had never been in Asia before and now, in two days, we would visit two countries. Not bad. We ate a bowl of cereal and headed out the door. This time we had mercifully less luggage, so that was very helpful. We got back into the familiar lines and waited in the familiar seats. It wasn't such a long flight, but we had a layover, so we were still traveling for most of the day.

As we arrived in Thailand, I was already struck with how clean it was. Also, how orderly and quiet. There were still lots of people and things were different than the States, but I felt much more at home in this place where people seemed to wait in line and no one was honking their horn. We were staying at a resort that had seen its best days about twenty years back. We spent a lot of our days in meetings while our kids were in child care. They seemed to be enjoying themselves and we, also, were having a good time meeting people and hearing stories. But, I really remember so little of that time because of . . . jet lag. It got so bad I wrote a song about it. In my life, if times get difficult enough, I write a song. Little did I know that I was about to encounter times in which even writing a song was more than I could do.

At all times in Thailand, I knew we were heading back to the Big City in eight days. It seemed an eternity during the nights and a whirlwind during the days, but soon enough, by God's grace, we were back on the plane to begin in earnest.

There was a time I hired a maid. The first morning I awoke in our new apartment hit by the incredible list of things I didn't know. Where were things in the house? Where could I buy things? How do I find a bus or taxi? Which way to a park for the kids to play in? Where am I, again? It's truly disconcerting to realize that you have no idea where you are or how to get the things you need. We had gotten some basic instructions from our friends. What we remembered from that jet-lag-laced conversation amounted to, "There's a Mother Dairy at the bottom of the hill and if you have questions, just ask Pearl." What was Mother Dairy? Hopefully we could get milk there. And who was this mysterious Pearl person?

We found some cereal in the house, but it was hard to eat cereal without milk, so we went on a quest for the Mother Dairy. Now, we happened to be at the top of a hill, so either way on the road led to the bottom. It didn't seem that we'd met with much to look at on the drive up the hill in one direction, so we headed down the hill in the opposite direction, hoping to find the land flowing with milk and honey — or at least something that resembled sugar? We arrived at a little garage-like store front where they sold milk in boxes or bags over a counter. We picked up some milk and wandered down the street, feeling completely bewildered. There were fabric shops, spice shops, vegetable sellers, dry goods vendors, and so many other things, but everything looked different from what we were used to and we hadn't brought much money with us. So, we picked up a few random things and hiked back up the hill. Carl on Bill's shoulders and James in the sling. We reached home, poured the boys some cereal and sat in front of the AC. That was about all we could handle that day.

The next day, however, Pearl arrived. It turned out that our friends who lent us their apartment had a house helper who came five days a week in the mornings to wash dishes, sweep, mop, and cook when needed. I was excited for the help, but completely bewildered as to how I should know what to ask her to do, or how to act with someone constantly in my home. Praise God for Pearl. She happened to be a believer. She happened to speak English. She happened to have worked for foreigners for most of her career. She happened to be willing to put up with my ignorance and help to steer me in the right direction. She, also, happened to know how to make mac and cheese and apple pie and chocolate chip cookies.

Now, I say that we hired her like it was no big deal. It was a big deal! I grew up on the farm. You do your own work, pull your own weight, grow your own food, fix your own plumbing, make your own meals, clean your own house, cut your own grass, do your own wash. Are you getting my point? Only the rich, snobby people hire help. If you can't do it yourself, you'd better learn how, hitch up your overalls, and get busy. That was always my way. I hated admitting I needed help from anyone.

At first, I had an easy excuse. If I didn't hire this lady, she'd be out of a job. It was only for a few months and I could learn a lot from her. It was culturally appropriate. I justified it in as many ways as I could without confessing one simple truth. I needed Pearl more than I could ever realize.

She would arrive in the morning and start on my pile of dishes. I never did the dishes unless I needed a specific bowl. I would just leave them stacked by the sink and she would take care of them every morning. She would sweep and mop and dust the entire house every day. It was so dusty in the city that this was absolutely necessary. So, despite her meticulous work, my kids were always covered in a layer of dust from playing on the marble floors that seemed to collect more as soon as it was swept up.

Even with the amazing help that Pearl brought to the family, I still struggled with having her in the house all the time. I felt that I couldn't completely relax. I couldn't discipline the kids without her making excuses for them and trying to quiet them with sugar. I wanted her to feel she could take a day off for a family need, but then, it seemed that the days off came more and more frequently. When should I put my foot down? I wanted something cooked or cleaned in a certain way, but it felt pushy to teach a woman who could be my mother how to do things. In the midst of trying to keep her on some kind of schedule, I came to look forward to her days off so I could let my hair down. I realized that I had a long way to go before I was comfortable with this new part of life here. If she had been any less honest, helpful, friendly, sweet, hard-working, or faithful, it would have been horrible. As it was, with a warm, wise, gentle, dependable woman, it was tolerable those first months. She got me through some difficult firsts and taught me how much I still needed to learn. I will never be able to repay this woman who became my Auntie for her tutelage.

In the U.S., you buy a dishwasher; you buy a food processor, you buy overpriced, pre-packaged food, you buy a vacuum and Swiffer Sweeper. Here, you hire a house helper. And, by God's grace, this person becomes an integral member of the family, a sister, a friend, and a person we could count on. God gave us Pearl.

There was a time when we walked two miles because of forty cents. We had been in the country for about a week or two. Right near where we lived was a really neat cultural site. Bill and I were excited to be in this new place, to learn all we could about it, and to expose our children to it all. So, we planned that on our day off we'd take our kids down the hill two miles to see it and then come back. It surely would be easy enough to get there and back and see a little bit of history.

That day, the high was easily 100 degrees. It was humid because of summer rains on the previous days. Fortunately, that day was sunny. We had to wait until at least 10:00 for the complex to open because nothing in our new city opened before 10-11 AM. So, after a 6:00 breakfast and trying to keep the boys occupied in the house for a few hours, we finally ventured out of the house, looking for an autorickshaw to bring us down the hill to the monument.

The auto wasn't hard to find and we squeezed into it with our boys, bottles of water, and high expectations. Arriving at the complex, it took us a while to find our way to the ticket counter where we encountered our first lesson in being a foreigner. A local could enter for fifty cents. It cost us eight dollars. Still, for the experience, it was well worth it to us. So, we found the entry gate and wandered through the crowd. It wasn't very packed by our city's standards, though it seemed so to us. Everywhere we looked, there were people on every patch of grass, under every tree, and of course, so many of them wanted pictures of our boys. Everyone in this new place wanted pictures of our boys. They were blue eyed and blonde haired. We made our way through the monuments in the complex, taking pictures of everything, trying to keep our sons from climbing on everything — and jumping off! We weren't sure what stuff was fair game and what stuff was sacred. To be fair, there were plenty of local kids jumping around, too, so we let up a bit and I ended up just following them around as they ran from brick to brick, step to step, tree to tree.

After Bill had taken enough photos, we decided we could go back. The sun was getting brutal and it was time for lunch. We walked out of the complex looking for an auto. The auto drivers looked excitedly at us — tourists! I could see the coins shining in their eyes. Tourists can be counted on to overpay. In our minds, though, we were not tourists. We were a family trying to become local. We were going to be here long term and wanted to be treated as such. So, when Bill asked the price and was given a ridiculous number, he scoffed. He walked away. Another auto tried a lower number, but it was still too high. We kept walking. It was only about two miles back to our apartment. We could walk it. At last, an auto gave a final offer. It was still almost double what it should have been. By this time, we were frustrated and disappointed. We wanted the fair rate. We wanted to be treated like locals. We wanted the acceptance of belonging. We'd already had to pay extra for the tickets. We wanted to get a good rate back up the hill. So, we walked on.

Carl walked for a bit, but then he got tired and hot. He never liked walking on the streets anyway. They were crowded. There were so many people and animals and vehicles coming at him and he couldn't see anything. Also, he got tired of dodging the dung in the streets. We were constantly telling him, "Look out! Don't step there!" His favorite question in that first month was, "Daddy, why is there so much poo here?" So, Bill would take him up on his shoulders so he could see. And, as I said before, it got him out of the way of the cheek-grabbers.

James was already snuggled into the sling on my hip. He was quickly dozing with the noise and motion and heat to lull him to sleep. So much for that afternoon nap I was counting on! Let's not forget that I was now five months pregnant. So, we traveled like this for the first relatively flat mile. No problem. Well, besides the heat. We were getting thirsty. Our water was empty. Bill started apologizing for not just taking the auto. As he calculated in his head what it would have cost and how far he was making his pregnant wife walk in the heat, carrying his son, he started to feel guilty. We got to the second half of the walk where the road went up. It got hotter. It got more crowded. We got more thirsty. We started looking for an auto, but by this time, I told Bill we might as well just walk it and get home. I had been as frustrated as he was and wouldn't have gotten into the auto anyway.

So, we trudged up the hill with our sleepy kids, wondering what we'd feed them when we got back home. I thought we might be able to find some cereal or leftover mac and cheese that Pearl had made for us. As we entered the blessed air conditioning of our flat, we went straight to the kitchen and poured some water for all of us. We sat at the table and Bill again apologized for making us walk up that hill. From that day on, he rarely argued with auto drivers. He didn't care so much about whether he got cheated and instead cared more about if his family arrived safely. I wish I could say the same. I still get my dander up when a driver quotes me a ridiculous price. Even if it's only a dollar.

Looking back, I can say it was pretty silly of me to think that my kids would get much out of this experience. Carl looked at the high tower and thought it was cool. James didn't see much of anything except faces of strangers trying to make him smile. I even thought it would be a good idea for my boys (aged one and a half and three) to have journals of all the exciting things they were experiencing. They've got about three pictures each in them — the number of times I actually had the energy to have the kids make a journal entry after an excursion. James' journal entry after that experience was a bunch of colorful scribbles. "I liked the steps," he told me when I eagerly asked him what was his favorite part of the ancient site. Carl told me he liked the ramp. You can almost make out a tower in his drawing. I still have those little sketchbooks in my pile of stuff. God gave us a new perspective on outings that day.

There was a day I learned to love the mall. Here we were, in a major tourist city for two months. We had language school five days a week, but we wanted to make the best of our time, and for sanity's sake, we needed to get the kids out of the house. So, several times a week, we tried to go on outings. Some of the lowest impact ones were to a park less than a mile from our flat. We walked down the busy road, through an open field littered with trash and animal dung, and down a path to a park/playground/archeological site. There were ruins of tombs/buildings and such in that park that dated back to around 1200 AD or so . . . that the kids could explore and climb around on! There were also wide open spaces with lots of grass where the kids could run and play. In one corner there was even, joy of all joys, a playground!

Now, don't get too excited. When I think of a playground, I think of nicely-kept metal/plastic/wooden equipment with a bed of sand/wood chips/pea gravel underneath to gently land a hazardous fall. This wasn't that. Imagine, if you will, a metal playground of the 80s. Imagine the steep slides, the sharp edges, and the complete lack of soft materials like wood and plastic. Now, imagine that no one had done any upkeep on that playground since the 80s. The paint is almost non-existent (and what is left is probably full of lead anyway). The metal is rusted and the slides have jagged holes in them, the climbing gym has pieces broken off and the screws are less-than-tightened. The swings look ready to come apart and the legs lift off the ground if you swing too high. Our kids loved it. And we did, too. It was over 100 degrees outside, but we needed those minutes away from the marble and concrete walls of our flat. We needed the kids to be able to run — even if they would arrive back home even more sweaty and dirty than when they left —if that was possible.

Besides our first attempt at the tourist site near our house, we also tried to visit a few more sites. I mean, we were in Asia, right? We'd get them dressed and pack a diaper bag (even though we were sure to find no bathrooms — let alone changing stations). We'd bring along several liters of water and a few snacks and set off on a grand adventure. We'd arrive at whatever interesting place it was and start to explore. But these outings turned out to be almost more stress for me than they were worth. We never had a time where we were out as a family without at least one to five hundred people looking at us. It got very tiring being the center of everyone's attention and feeling the need to protect my children and help them feel safe. We went from trying to go out several times a week as a family to just taking quick trips to the park early in the morning before many people were up and about. This turned out to be the best practice for us.

Another surprising discovery was that I loved the mall. Who'd-a-thunk? The mall became our go-to spot for a getaway. There was air conditioning. Most of the people there spoke English. There were restaurants and shops that we recognized. And, best of all, there was a playground inside with plastic, clean, safe equipment. It was even free!! So, we would walk down the hill, through our crazy market to the bus stand. I only knew one number of bus in the city — the bus that would take us to the mall. We'd jump on with the kids and I would hope that someone would see my pregnant belly and our little kids and give up their seat. Usually they would, but sometimes I'd be left hanging onto a seat back trying to keep James on my hip and reassuring Carl that he wouldn't get crushed before reaching the stop at the mall. If I had tried to clean myself or the kids up before we headed to the mall, it didn't make much difference. By the time we got there, we were so sweaty and dusty it looked like we'd just finished working in the fields. We didn't care. We were about to eat donuts and french fries!

We'd hop off the bus and walk up to the mall, through the metal detectors, and then through the doors. A wave of cool air would wash over us as strains from a familiar song played over the loud speakers. We'd herd our boys onto the playground equipment. One of us would watch the kids while the other one went and got some coffee. We'd revel in the clean, cool air until lunchtime, get some fast food, and make our way back down the escalators, back into the oppressive heat, back on the crowded bus, and back up the tumultuous hill to our flat. The stark contrast between the mall and our day-to-day reality hit hard. Even our local playground and the mall playground were such a contrast in the very same city. God gave us an unexpected sanctuary of sorts in the midst of all the chaos.

There was a time when we prayed away a bulldozer. Ellen was our language tutor. She lived in a slum just a few blocks from the flat we were renting during our time in the Big City. Our primary goals were to get used to the culture and learn some of the language before we moved out to the more remote city that would be our first home. Ellen taught Bill and I and three other Americans how to speak a new language without using any English. She didn't know any. It was an exciting way for me to learn and an exasperating way for Bill. I loved the ambiguity of it all and started catching on to the phrasing and grammar and sounds while Bill struggled to remember simple words. Ellen was quick to point this out. In a culture where shaming students is completely normal, she would look at her student and say, "Your wife is learning this so easily. You are the dumbest one in the class." Bill would swallow these insults, smile, and try harder. He knew that if they didn't fall on him, they would fall on the next worst student in the class. He was willing to be the scapegoat.

This didn't mean that Ellen disliked Bill. On the contrary, he was really her favorite student. They would joke together and it seemed that she really wanted him to understand. This was just the only motivation she knew of. She invited us all to her home for a festival and introduced us to her kids. She was conscientious and almost never missed class. One day, she seemed out of sorts. At our tea break, we asked how things were going. She told us that bulldozers had come to her community this morning and were going to start tearing down the houses. All the houses in the slum were illegal structures. She and her family were squatting along with about 5000 other people. The government had issued them warnings about leaving, but this had happened before. This was the first time that the bulldozers had actually come. Her older daughter was at home alone, waiting to see what would happen. Her younger daughter had gone to school and her son was at work. What could they do against the bulldozers? So she came to work. At least she could make some money today.

Our class was horrified. We asked if we could pray with her and for her and the community. We prayed in English and we prayed in her language. She prayed, too. After the prayers, we sent her home. Who cared about the new list of words to learn when she might lose her house that day. The rest of the day, I was consumed with thoughts of this woman who had become our friend and mentor. Would her little girl come home to a flattened house? Would they be able to get their few belongings out of the house before it came down? Where would they sleep tonight? I prayed some more.

That night we got a phone call from a friend who also knew Ellen and her family. The house was safe. The government had decided to give everyone in the community two weeks to find other housing before they flattened the homes. Ellen and her family had time to move their belongings and find a better and safer place. We were thrilled! The next day when Ellen came to class, we asked her about her home. Her eyes shined. She was so thankful for the prayers and knew that God had spared her family. We asked her about her plans. Where would she move? When would she move? How could we help? "Oh, I'm not moving. The government might forget about all this. I have no where else to go. I just have to hope for the best."

I couldn't believe it. I couldn't imagine a life where I just kept living, waiting for the bulldozers to come back and finish the job. My life had taught me to act to preserve what was mine. My life had taught me that my efforts mattered. My life had taught me that I had choices. I caught a glimpse into Ellen's life. Her life had taught her that she had no choices, that her efforts didn't matter, that her actions didn't matter. I could see a bit more clearly what it meant to live in a slum . . . hoping the government would forget about you.

I wish I could say the government did forget. But it didn't. Another day, a few months later, the bulldozers came and didn't stop. They flattened many houses in that community and took off half of Ellen's house. The last I knew of her family, they were still living in the half of the house that remained standing. At least there was a roof over their heads. God spared a room for her family and she gave thanks to him for it.

Kite City

These first few months were a whirlwind. God had a lot to introduce my heart to. I had started to get used to the dust and heat, the crowds and noise. We always knew that this first home would be temporary. We were preparing to move to Kite City. We took a trip out to visit before our move. As we traveled on the slightly-paved roads out to the smaller city, I breathed a sigh of relief. I saw fields, farm animals, farmers, small villages with small houses. This felt more like home. I was used to farmers. I was used to fields and open spaces. It was the first time I had seen so much space since we arrived and it felt freeing. I thought, "If this is where we're headed, I can do this." I had so much more to learn. This new city was smaller, yes, but it was also more remote. There were less places for the kids to play. There was no house helper who spoke English and knew how to make chocolate chip cookies. There was a smaller home with almost no furniture. There were no malls to escape to. Besides all this, in our new city, people were even less accustomed to seeing foreigners. I was not prepared for this new, even more alienating environment. Thankfully, God was. He knew that my initial relief of leaving the Big City would fade. He knew what challenges awaited us in Kite City. He was ready with the grace for these challenges.

There was a time my best friend knocked on my door and introduced herself. We had arrived in Kite City. We lugged our children and crates onto the elevator and up to the third floor of our apartment building. We took stock of the closet space, living space, and shelf space. We started to unpack several boxes while our boys napped in the back room on their new beds. I was wavering between cautious optimism and total despair, hoping for what might be and cringing at the seemingly impossible task of settling in to another completely new environment. Suddenly, there was a knock at the door.

We weren't expecting anyone yet, but maybe one of our foreign friends had wanted to check in with us. Maybe the caretaker of the apartment building had some business for us. I quickly grabbed my head scarf, flung it over my head, and answered the door. There stood a sweet, young, local woman with a round, smiling face, sparkling eyes, and impeccable English, "Hello, my name is Nada. I was wondering if you could use a language tutor. I worked for the woman who used to live here." I could hardly catch my breath. I had prayed and prayed that God would lead me to the right language tutor, to people who could be true friends in this land where we were foreigners and outsiders. Here stood the answer to my prayers in under an hour.

I hastily invited her in and Bill went to make some tea so we could talk more freely. I cleared some space on one of the couches that we hadn't planned on keeping. They had wooden edges and loud, patterned cushions. There were also glass-covered tables. Pretty much a disaster waiting to happen with our two active boys around. But we hadn't gotten them moved out yet, so I was able to welcome this new neighbor in style before we changed to mats folded on the floor for seating and a tablecloth spread on the marble floor for meals.

We exchanged particulars. I told her that, yes, I was looking for language help. She quoted me a more-than-fair price. She also told me that her house helper was looking for more work and might want to work for me. So I ended up hiring Joy, a sweet, steady, faithful, and fun girl, to help with cooking and cleaning tasks in the house. All this happened within the first half hour of her visit. Even with the particulars out of the way, she stayed on.

We chatted about our families, our hopes and dreams, our faith, our struggles. She was so candid and comfortable with me that I felt we had known each other forever. After she shared some particularly difficult circumstances she was facing, I asked if I could pray for her in Jesus' name. She agreed. I prayed and we continued talking for about three total hours. After she left, I looked around at all the boxes that still needed unpacking, the floor that still needed sweeping, the family that still needed feeding, and I wept thankful tears of joy. I knew this young woman would be my best friend in the area. I knew that she would be such an encouragement in a place where few others spoke any English, where I was still floundering to understand basic conversation, where I understood so little about the community.

The next day, mid-morning, I heard a knock again. There was Nada, smiling, asking if I had time to chat. I gladly opened the door and, through morning routine and crazy kids' antics, we continued our conversation from the day before. This became a regular occurrence. I ended up not getting a lot of language study done because we would start in the local language, but pretty soon one of us would switch to English to tell a joke or ask a deep question and our lesson would be over. The cultural lessons I gleaned from her, however, were priceless. And the time we spent getting out into the community together, meeting some of her distant relatives, and hashing out deep conversations was well worth it.

That second day, though, she said something that stayed with me. "I want to tell you something that may sound very strange. Something happened to me yesterday. I think your prayers really work." I beamed at my new friend. "Nada, that's why I pray!" I spoke those words a little too enthusiastically. There would be days where I wondered if my prayers were doing any good at all, if God was truly listening. But God gave me an answer to my prayer for a friend in the first hour. I would go back to that day and remind myself of this when the answers were coming more slowly. God gave me my hearts desire at just the right time, and God gave Nada glimpses into His love for her. He taught her that she could pray, too, trusting that He was listening.

There was a time when my morning devotional was interrupted by someone's morning constitutional. Well, many times, in fact. When we moved into our new apartment in Kite City, we were thrilled. We actually had a view. There was a big hospital complex where some new buildings were under construction right off our balcony. That meant that there was a big grassy lot and a little pond (cess pool) in our view instead of a side of a building. I loved the idea that we could look out our window, or even sit on our balcony, and see out over the rooftops of the town. It was a great comfort after being surrounded by tall buildings in the Big City.

It was still oppressively hot when we arrived, but the mornings would sometimes be a bearable 85 degrees. Bill and I would pour our coffee, pull a plastic chair onto the balcony, and sit with our Bibles and devotionals and journals. We usually had to take turns because the boys would be up. So one of us would wrangle the kids and get them breakfasted while the other took a little 'quiet' time.

Now, quiet was always a relative term in our home. If it wasn't the sound of tractors moving dirt behind the house, it was stray dogs barking or the mosques blaring the call to prayer or motorcycles honking or vendors yelling. But early in the morning, after the call to prayer was over, it was relatively quiet. People weren't typically working yet and the dogs had been fighting all night and were taking their morning naps. So it was the calmest — and coolest — time of day.

Sitting out on the balcony could feel almost isolated. No one else sat on their balconies and we weren't facing the street. I was settling into my journal, sipping my coffee, when a man walked down the lane towards the construction site and made a bee-line for the field. "What's going on here?" I thought. Then I found out. Most labor-class people in India don't have a bathroom at home. They have to find a quiet field somewhere to do what they need to do. There are no public facilities for them. In a village, this can be a lot easier — people will just go outside the village. But in a city, any unkept piece of land becomes the community latrine.

Our beautiful balcony faced the laborers' morning stop. Soon, there were a few other men, then a few women. Each found their own corner of the field. At the time, I didn't know what to do. Should I go back inside? This was my balcony and the only place I could escape the craziness of my toddlers for a little moment with my Lord. Should I move my book so it shielded my eyes from the field? After a while, there were too many people and not enough books. I figured they just didn't know I was there. Usually people didn't sit on their balconies and I was quiet enough that they might not have noticed me. But then one person looked up, saw me, and still made his way to the field. I figured if they knew I was there, they would find somewhere else to go. I didn't really think about the fact that they had nowhere else.

I can now imagine their shock that this woman just kept sitting there. Who did she think she was? But how was I going to get any time with Jesus if I didn't have my coffee on the balcony? After a few days of this, I gave up. I couldn't very well ignore what was happening below me and they didn't seem to be changing their position any, so I resigned and went back inside. From that time on, as long as we lived in Kite City, I had my 'quiet' time in my bedroom with the door locked. I could hear every comment from every member of my family. I could hear every whine from my kids. I could hear the knocks on the door when they wanted in. There was never an uninterrupted morning time again. But God still fed me, even when I had no place of my own to meet with Him.

There was a time I yelled at a journalist. Our children made quite a spectacle. They were small. They were cute. They were blonde. They were blue-eyed. They were foreign. It was pretty impossible to hide in the sea of brown-skinned, dark-haired people who made up our neighborhoods. Within the first week, we learned how difficult it was going to be to have any kind of an outing with our family and maintain any amount of anonymity. At restaurants, people would walk up to our table and ask to "snap just one pic" with our kids. Walking on the street, other families would point our kids out to their kids and try to get them to practice the English phrases they were taught in school or try to make them hold hands for a photo, even if their child and our child wanted nothing to do with it. It was exhausting. All we wanted was to just be able to get out of the house without becoming the main attraction. To this day, it still hasn't happened.

One day, after we had moved to our new city, another foreign family and I decided we'd take our kids (and our pregnant bellies) to a local park we'd heard about. It was even rumored that there were slides and swings! What a luxury! What we didn't realize was that it happened to be one of many school holidays. When we arrived at the park on our rickshaws, we found the playground equipment covered in school-age boys. About forty kids between the ages of six and twelve were running around, climbing on everything. Well, since we were there, we'd try to do our best.

As soon as we walked into the area, we were surrounded by the boys. Some were polite while others were rude. There wasn't a single parent in sight and we found ourselves trying to referee a hoard of kids who all wanted a piece of our children. They tried to pick them up, push them on the swings, carry them to the slides, talk to them, and touch their hair, hands, faces, etc. Carl started to get really upset. The other kids didn't like it either. We finally had to grab our kids and run to the opposite end of the park to escape all the attention. As we made our getaway, I had to rudely yell at the boys to make them stay where they were and not follow us around. I didn't have good enough language skills to say what I wanted, so it came out, "No, not nice, go away, go home!"

We settled ourselves into a quieter lawn where there was a space of green grass to play in. The kids started throwing around baseballs with their friend's Dad when a strange man walked up with a fancy camera. "Can I take a picture of your family?"

I reverted to a phrase I was told would work in this culture. "I'm sorry, my husband isn't here to ask. No, you may not." There, that would manage.

But he persisted, "I'm with the local newspaper. I'm doing a piece on the holiday. Just one pic." Gosh, this was going to be harder than I thought.

I mustered up my most stern, teacher, I-mean-what-I-say face and said, "Absolutely not. My husband is not here. Leave us alone now."

Well, after a few more interchanges like this, he finally moved away and I figured I'd won. I started watching my kids happily playing, oblivious to the interaction I was having and hopefully, to the stares of all the other park-goers and passers-by. But my joy was short-lived as I turned around and saw this newspaper man lying on the grass with a super-zoom lens pointed straight at my kids. At this point Mama Bear snapped. I didn't really think. I just walked and started yelling in a mixture of English and the local language. "I said,'NO!' Get out of here with your camera! How dare you! Go away!" He kept on shooting while I walked towards him, yelling. Finally, he got up, put his lens cap on, and started moseying away, like a crazy foreign lady was not yelling at him the whole time. I'm not sure if it was the shaming that finally did it or if he was afraid of what I'd do if I actually reached him.

At this point, I was exhausted. I just wanted to take my kids home and hide. So that's what I did. We hailed a rickshaw, squeezed onto the seat, and bumped our way home to our dusty, hot, barren sanctuary. This was not the first or the last time I felt ambushed by all the attention, but I've gotten more used to it. I adopted a policy of "ask the kids." If they wanted to stand for a picture then they could. If they didn't, I'd guard them with my life. I have stared down people trying to pretend they're playing on their phone while trying to take photos of my kids in public places. I've patiently waited while James posed with six to ten young women who thought he was "too cute!" even when I was running late. And I've scolded a shepherd boy trying to take our picture while carrying a baby goat. By God's grace, I haven't smashed any cameras . . . yet.

There was a time when I had an OB-GYN exam with three other patients in the room with me. We were very optimistic about having a home birth in our new city. Our first two babies were born without complications or drugs, so we figured we could have a home birth. We found a midwife who was willing to drive the three and a half hours to our home when we called her to tell her the baby was coming. All we needed now was to find a hospital nearby that we could rush to if there were any complications. Just in our backyard was the government hospital complex. I figured this would be the perfect place — easy to get to in an emergency. I decided to have a visit there beforehand, just to find out about the place.

I asked Nada to go with me to help with translating, if need be. We arrived and I had to buy a ticket for about a quarter. This gave me the number I needed to see one of the OB doctors. We sat down in the waiting room to . . . wait. There were about fifty other women there with family members or spouses. A few of them struck up conversations with me and I realized that most of these women had traveled quite a distance from the surrounding villages. This was the only hospital they could afford and probably the only check-up they would receive before giving birth. Some young men — probably medical interns — were calling out numbers. After about half an hour, my name was called and then we had to wait in a line with about ten other patients. At this point, there was a gurney in the hallway with soiled sheets on it. Eventually a woman was laid on this gurney and taken out of the rooms. I was trying not to imagine what it would be like to be that woman.

We finally entered the doctor's office and it was so chaotic I didn't know where to turn. There were about four desks piled high with papers and orderlies, nurses, interns, etc. going from desk to desk, speaking quickly. I understood none of it. Finally, an intern looked at me and asked me some questions in broken English and then motioned for me to walk into an examination room. I pulled back the curtain to find a patient on the table in the middle of an examination. Several other women were waiting against the wall in this crowded room which was about the size of a walk-in closet. A bucket with water and used instruments was standing in the corner. I just tried to find something to look at that didn't make me uncomfortable.

Settling on Nada's face, I tried smiling at her. She grabbed my hand and looked scared herself. She was single and had never had a need to enter a place like this. When it was my turn, the doctor just had me sit on the table, asked me a few questions, measured my stomach, and sent me back to the office room. There, a man gave me a prescription for some pills I didn't understand, told me I had to have a bunch of blood work done, and sent me on my way. I was flustered, but tried not to be.

There are things you experience when you are in the middle of culture stress that don't register until after you are out of the situation. As we rode home, my friend asked me lots of questions about what it was like to be pregnant, what examinations were like, and would she have to do these things some day if God answered her prayers and gave her a husband and children. No one else in her life would speak to her about these things. Her mother was dead and an unmarried woman is not supposed to talk about or know about such things. As I spoke with her, I realized just how difficult what I saw had been. The interns and nurses and doctors treated the women more like animals than people. No one explained anything to any of them and they never had a chance to ask any questions. I had numerous books at my disposal to help me through the trials of pregnancy and delivery. Many of those women probably couldn't even read, let alone find books that could help them.

After I arrived home, I talked to Bill about what I had seen and heard. I started to tell him I wanted to try to find a private hospital nearby that was a little less crowded and a little more clean. As I told him, I started to cry. He just held me as I wept for all the women I had seen at the hospital. They didn't have other options. If they were lucky enough to have a doctor attend their birth at all, it would be in a place like that. If not, the birth would be at home with an untrained midwife or a few relatives in attendance. I had all the choices at my fingertips. I could travel to another city and give birth in a fancy hospital. I could even fly to the States if I was concerned. I could have a trained midwife in my own home. These women had nowhere else to go and didn't know anything different. I cried for them. I cried for their daughters. I prayed for a way for women to have a different experience than the one I'd seen. God gave me the gift of empathy that day — empathy for the millions and, probably, billions of women who never had and never will have a choice.

There was a time we crossed the border while I was eight months pregnant. Our visa stipulated that we had to leave the country every six months. We had only been in the country four months, but our baby was due in another month and we weren't sure we would have the passport and visa for our new kid by the time we'd need to leave. We decided it made more sense to take a trip now and give ourselves more time to get the paperwork together. I was too far along now in my pregnancy to fly, so we looked at a map and saw that there was a border that we could cross by car not too far from where we were — only about 180 miles. This was a little over half the distance we used to drive from our home to our family when we lived in the States. Sure, the roads would be worse and more crowded and a land-border crossing might be a bit confusing, but that was nothing to worry about. We could probably do it in about five hours, spend the night, and come back the following day. We started preparing our family for the 'Adventure.'

Our kids soon learned this was our code word for any upcoming ordeal that we really didn't know anything about. If there was the possibility or likelihood of being delayed, uncomfortable, stranded, sick, etc., we called it an 'Adventure.' So we packed extra diapers, extra clothes, extra wet-wipes, extra snacks, and extra prayers and set off in the early morning to try to reach the border. We had heard that there were several times each day that the border would open for cars. We were planning to cross the border shortly after lunch and then make our way to a hotel where we could relax for the rest of the day and drive back early the next morning. We'd get home in the early afternoon. Adventure Time.

Our first observation was that our trip included the singularly worst maintained road that we had ever ridden on. This was saying something. There were more pot-holes in the road than there was road. This led to car sick boys and a pretty pained Mama. The boys wanted to sit on my lap or lean on me, would fall asleep on me in various positions, or would cry and whine until Bill took them up in the front with him. I would try to keep my focus outside so that I wouldn't get car sick, too. We stopped once or twice along the way for the men to go to the bathroom on the side of the road. I kept telling myself that I could hold it until we reached the hotel. As we continued on, though, and checked our GPS against the clock, we realized that our five hour drive was very quickly turning into an eight hour drive. We were going to miss the border opening by at least an hour. As we rolled up to the bridge used for the crossing, it was more than obvious that we were too late. Our driver pulled under a tree so there would at least be some shade and we pulled out some snacks. We let the boys get out of the car, thinking that they could run around and let off steam while we waited the extra three hours before the next open gate. Pretty soon, though, we were calling them back into the car as we realized that the entire side of the road was covered in a thick layer of dust. Dust on the grass, on the stones, on the trees, and now all over my boys.

After a few minutes of this, I heard a school bell ring. Out of a building nearby swarmed class after class of students. It didn't take them long to notice the SUV under the tree with a bunch of foreign folks in it. We soon became the zoo. Kids just surrounded the car and stared into the windows. The driver told them once or twice to leave, but of course, they didn't. We just sat there not knowing what to do. Then, a couple of the older boys started laughing and pointing at my belly and joking together. That was the last straw. I unrolled my window and in my best local language yelled, "Bad talk! Bad boys! Go to your Mama!" They were shocked and shamed and slowly started walking. When they left, everyone else started leaving too. We had a fairly quiet hour to rest as we waited for the border to open. It was during this time that the driver pulled out his license, asking if it was valid. We couldn't read the script, but Bill was pretty sure it was expired. The driver kept telling us not to worry.

My bladder gave up and I had to try to find somewhere to go to the bathroom. Our driver went looking for me and came back telling me to follow him. He introduced me to a lady from a farm house on the roadside. She quietly and politely led me to a grove of trees behind her house and motioned, 'there.' She turned around and left, so I looked for the most hidden spot and did what all farm girls have learned to do.

Back at the car, we were thrilled when we saw the line of vehicles start moving. We got through the gate and over the bridge only to reach several booths we needed to visit before we could continue. Our driver helped Bill navigate these as we paid some money which we weren't quite sure whether it was for taxes, fees, or bribes. Then we had to get our entry visa. Bill knocked on the shop door and was told by a very inebriated man that it was too late and he'd have to come back tomorrow morning. 7:30? No! At least 10:30. That meant we were going to miss the early morning crossing. It also meant that we were going to spend the night at the hotel without an entry visa.

We piled back into the car and headed to the hotel. They had no room for drivers, so we purchased another room for him. Then, we finally made our way to our room — it was already after our kids' bedtime. Carl decided to throw a royal screaming fit on the way to the room. I don't remember what it was about, but I remember carrying him, kicking and screaming, through the hotel room door. We stopped to gain our bearings, pray, cry, and laugh. Then, we went downstairs to try to get some dinner. As we ate, I saw mice scuffling under the tables and as we walked back to our room, I saw several dead cockroaches — at least they were dead!

The next morning, we ate breakfast, prayed for mercy, and headed back to the visa office. Surprisingly, the man was there and was able to give us an entry visa just in time for us to turn around and go to the exit visa office. We then had to wait until noon when the border opened up. We watched school children walking to school, men on bikes piled with goods, and all manner of trucks and tractors, animals and people.

All of a sudden, I had to poo. There was NO WHERE to go. We couldn't get out of our place in the line of cars to try to find somewhere, so I got out of the car and started scanning the roadside. The border is a river. I looked around the river bank and there were a few scraggly bushes. They were barely a screen for my bottom half, but they'd have to do. I maneuvered my pregnant belly and managed. After getting back to the car, I resolved to drink and eat as little as possible until we reached home.

As the border gate opened, we squeezed back over the bridge and found our way back down the same roads we had just seen the day before. We reached the pothole stretch and I breathed a sigh of thanks as the sun began to set. We were getting close. But then it got dark and I saw that we still had two hours to go — dodging buses, pedestrians, stray animals, carts, motorcycles with families on them, and all manner of other travelers. I gasped a prayer of protection and tried to close my eyes and trust. Bill will often say it was the most dangerous drive we'd ever undertaken. About this time, our driver reminded us that wild elephants and tigers still lived in the woods on either side of the road we were traveling on. Well, that was reassuring. Still, God's grace got us home. We carried our sleeping kids up the steps, since the power was out and the elevator wasn't working. We opened the door and dropped them onto their mats. God brought us through our first border crossing without any accidents . . . of any kind.

6

There was a day I thought I was having a baby. I had such a great plan for how we would welcome our third child into our family. We wanted to have the baby in our city — I mean, half a million women lived there and had their babies there, so I figured it was good enough for me, too. After having gone to the government hospital, though, we knew we needed a different option for an emergency situation. We found a smaller, private hospital not far from our home where the doctor seemed knowledgeable and open to having me come and deliver there. We didn't tell them that we planned on a home birth and would only be there in an emergency. That wouldn't have made any sense to them.

We put everything in place. I had my midwife and her assistant on standby. All I had to do was call them when we were pretty sure that it was time. We had a friend who was ready to take our boys to their home when the time came. One of my other friends had agreed to come and be with Bill and I until the midwives could get there and to assist Bill with the delivery if the midwives didn't make it in time. She even came over while the midwife did a check-up on me and she and Bill practiced giving each other shots so that they could inject me with Pitocin right after the birth if they had to. Now that's what I call true love! We also had another friend who would wait with a car just in case we needed to get to the hospital quickly. Everything was running so smoothly!

Two days after my due date, my contractions started. I was having fairly hard, fairly regular, and fairly painful contractions for a few hours when I decided we'd better call the midwife. I really didn't want to risk my midwife not being there, so we started the ball rolling. It really did feel like when I'd had my other two kids. I also called my friend who came over as soon as she could. We didn't bring the boys to the other house yet since we didn't know how long I'd be in labor and I didn't want them to wear out their welcome.

The midwife arrived at my house about three and a half hours later. The contractions were strong but weren't getting stronger. They were regular but weren't getting closer together. We waited. We talked. My midwife suggested I go for a walk to try to speed things up or kick them into gear. My friend and I walked all the way to and through the market. We walked to another friend's house at least a mile away. She was shocked to see me, "Aren't you supposed to be having a baby?!" Yes, that's what I thought, too. We walked all the way back to the house. The contractions got stronger as we walked, but as soon as we got back home, they weakened again. We waited. It was nighttime. My midwife and her assistant would spend the night. Things would probably pick up after dark. They didn't. I laid down to sleep and the contractions slowed and then stopped. I was so frustrated! And tired!

In the morning, I said goodbye to the midwives. There was no point in them staying. They needed to get home to their own kids. Before they left, they told me that they wouldn't be able to come all that way again. I understood. One of them had a kid back home that was nursing. I told them not to worry and we'd just have the baby in the local hospital we had found. I was so disappointed. We had EVERYTHING in place, EVERYTHING was perfect, and that baby just wouldn't show up! Now what?

Bill and I decided we'd better set up another appointment with the doctor at the hospital — just to make sure things were going to be okay. When I was eight days past my due date, we had our appointment. The doctor checked me. She was pushing that I be induced because I was so 'late'. I didn't want that. She told me I should get another ultrasound just to check and make sure the baby was okay. I agreed to that. Bill started to press her about his presence in the birthing room. Typically, in Kite City, men aren't with their wives when they give birth. So it was a strange request, but we felt very firm about Bill needing to be there. The nurses spoke little English, it was a strange place and culture (we'd only been in the country for four months!), and I would need his support. The doctor started to backpedal saying it wasn't normal, but 'God willing' he would be allowed. Well, Bill told her that he knew that God wanted him there, but what would she allow? He pushed and pushed her until she admitted that she didn't feel comfortable with him in the room. We smiled, told her we understood, and walked out of the hospital never to walk back in.

Bill turned to me, "We've got to get to the Big City. Now!" We knew that there were hospitals there that were used to foreigners and our weird ways. We knew that we could find somewhere to deliver there. Our midwife lived there and would probably be able to help us. We realized just how naive we were to think that we could have the birthing experience we wanted in this city. We started to pray and plan. We still had an ultrasound appointment and figured that it might be a help to have that paperwork when we went to another hospital, so we went to the ultrasound lab. On the way, I started feeling some mild contractions. I wrote it off to the stress of the situation and tried to relax.

At the ultrasound lab, the technician had some more difficult news. "Your baby is measuring about 5 weeks small. It is lethargic. You should induce labor or have a c-section." At first, I was freaked out. What was I going to do? So I called my midwife for her advice. She calmed me down, reminding me that she'd seen me only a few days before, that the baby was a good size, and that ultrasounds can be mistaken. She also reminded me that our baby might have been sleeping. I calmed down. I started to wonder if the ultrasound tech was in league with the doctor we'd just visited.

We made our way back home and started calling everyone we knew. Was there a place we could stay? Our friends in the Big City all were out of town or had guests already visiting them. We tried hotels, but it turned out that there was a big event in the city that weekend. Also, as my contractions continued and strengthened, I began to worry that we wouldn't make it to a hospital and might be having a home birth somewhere after all. I tried to play them off to Bill. He was already stressed out enough. Finally, a friend who had turned us down called us back. "We know it's probably not even an option, but our family has an unfurnished flat they are trying to sell and you could use it for a few days." Perfect! We started packing.

We called our driver friend and by God's grace, he was free to drive us. When Bill called his language helper, Ethan, to tell him we were going, he insisted on coming with us. "My Sister will make it safely to that flat. I will be sure of it." We gathered mats for the floor, portable cribs for the boys, clothes, food, dishes, toys, baby things, the home birth kit . . . basically our whole house. As we did so, I had to excuse myself to sit down every once in a while, "Don't worry, Honey, it's nothing. Probably just stressed out, that's all." Yeah, right.

As we crowded into the car and took off down the road, I was struck by how things didn't work out like I'd expected. This was not what I'd wanted. God had His own plans and was sending us on our way to have our baby.

7

There was a day I had my third boy. We were bumping along the road to the Big City. Our driver was in the front seat sustaining some small talk with Bill's language helper in the passenger seat. Bill was next to me in the back seat — a welcome change since he usually sat in front and I was left with the kids in the back by myself. James was sleeping on my lap and Carl was sleeping, leaning against my side. I was in labor. Now, it was so bad I couldn't speak through the contractions. I had to force myself not to cry out in pain. Our escorts had never been around a woman in labor before and it was completely inappropriate for that to happen. So, I pretended I wasn't in labor. A few miles back, I had told Bill that he'd better call our midwife and see if she and her assistant could meet us at the unfurnished flat that would be our home for the next week. The baby was coming soon.

I started to feel sorry for myself: a woman traveling on a bumpy road, trying to get to an unfurnished flat to deliver a baby. Then I realized, being that it was December fourteenth, I knew of another woman who had needed to deliver a baby on a journey. I was in an SUV bumping down a road. Mary had been on a donkey. I was going to an unfurnished flat. Mary was going to a stable. I didn't really have it so bad.

We reached the flat and I grabbed James to carry him up the stairs. I think at that point someone took him. I remember having a contraction on the way to the flat and trying to pretend I wasn't. Our friends met us there and let us in. They hugged us while our driver and Ethan left. We put the boys to bed in a far room and I started arranging the mats in the front room where I would deliver. I'd stop every once in a while to have another contraction. My midwife arrived to find me sitting in a chair while Bill recounted all the events of the last twelve hours to the delight of our friends. I was still trying to act like I wasn't in as much pain as I was. One of our friends was videotaping the whole exchange. Looking back at the video, Bill could see my face as I labored there on the chair with the videotaper's wife rubbing my shoulders. "I'm so sorry! I had no idea you were already so far!" I guess I had done a good job of hiding it.

My midwife walked in, took one look at me, and said, "You go in there (pointing at the front room) and I'll dismiss the crowds." I thanked her, hugged our friends, and made my way to the mat. I didn't leave that mat for six hours. After the craziness and stress of the day, I had nothing left. I couldn't do all the things I was supposed to do to help the labor progress. I can remember praying that God would please help this baby come before the boys woke up. What would we do if the boys woke up?

They tried to make the room as comfortable as possible. We had one space heater — the temperature was near freezing that night — but it wasn't putting out much heat. We had blankets covering the large windows, but they weren't quite covered, so we kept the lights off in the house. We didn't think the neighbors would want a front row seat to all that was about to take place!

At around 4 AM, I started to panic. I had no energy and the baby wasn't coming. My midwife asked if I could eat something. Bill brought me some juice and toast with jam. I ate and tried to sit up but kept falling back on the bed. I started asking Bill what we were thinking . . . telling him that I didn't think I could make it.

At about 5:15, I sat straight up in bed, clapped my hands, and pumped my fists. "Let's do this!" I can imagine Bill and the midwife laughing. I was ready and so was the baby. About that time, we heard Carl crying in his port-a-crib. Bill went to encourage him to fall back asleep for a bit longer. He came back and I started to deliver the baby. As the baby was coming out, James started to cry and Carl poked his head into the room. Bill threw Carl his phone and told him to go play Angry Birds for a few minutes. Carl left just as Bill caught the baby, declaring, "It's a boy! We've got Caleb!" We rushed to wrap the baby against the cold. We invited the boys into the room to meet their brother. I fed Caleb and wrote him a song as I held him. Bill held him and blessed him to be 'strong and courageous' just like Caleb in the Bible.

We were enjoying our little boy so much! The midwife was making records of the birth. We called our family to tell them the good news. Bill's Dad was at a funeral, so he mass-texted the family and shut off his phone for six hours. The sun was well-up and it was getting warmer in the room. It was time to clean off, weigh, and measure the baby. I handed Caleb to the midwife. She unwrapped the warm towel and gasped. Bill gasped. "Uh, Mag . . . it's a girl! We've got Josie!" What???!!! In the craziness, cold, dark, and rush, no one had thought to check if Bill was right.

I have never given him a hard time about this. The only person who had a more stressful day than him was me. At that time, we had to start getting used to this new family member. We had to tell the boys they had a sister. We had to tell the family in America that we had a daughter. Some of them got confused thinking we were saying we had twins. Finally, we got it all sorted out. Josie got her blessing from Daddy. I wrote a song for Josie. We hugged and snuggled her. We were thrilled with her. By God's grace, we had our little girl.

8

There was a day I swept the floor after giving birth. We were so grateful the day Josie was born. It had been so strange and amazing and chaotic, but there was our beautiful baby, safe and sound, healthy and strong. She could already raise her head and push herself up from the floor. She even rolled from one side to the other in that first week. I'm sure she didn't try to, but she was that strong. All of us had taken turns holding her, singing to her, smelling her baby hair, looking at her baby hands and feet. We were just so thankful.

After the newness settled in, we realized that we were in an unfurnished flat with two young boys (Carl was three and a half and James was not yet two) and a baby. We knew we had to stick around for a few days to try to work things out with paperwork. Josie needed an authorized birth certificate, a health check, and an application for a passport. We wanted to make sure that we got this started so we could then begin work on the visa. Also, I wasn't too thrilled with the idea of traveling back home just yet. That ride didn't sound very appealing. Just the same, it didn't sound too appealing to hang out in an unfurnished flat for several days. Bill decided he'd take the boys on a scouting trip around the neighborhood looking for the nearest markets and playground, if only to get them out of the house so the baby and I could sleep.

They headed out the door. I nursed our daughter, and she fell sweetly asleep in my arms. That's when the nesting kicked in. Usually, mothers do this before their babies come. They want their homes to be just right to welcome the little bundle of joy. But, all my nesting had been done at our flat three and a half hours away. In the hours before her birth, nesting was not my top priority! So, I started looking around. There were dirty dishes in the sink, things scattered around, and above all, the floor was filthy. The floor looked like it had been swept before we arrived, probably by our friends, but it probably also had weeks of dust on it before that. I could see the layer of dust still sitting on the floor, as well as what we'd tracked in from our arrival. I just couldn't stand thinking about my little baby in this dirty place. It's not like there was a couch or chairs to sit on to keep her up off the floor. We were right there, on our mats, right next to it all the time. I looked around, found the broom, cleared the clutter, and started sweeping.

Now, I figure that most smart people would tell me, "Maggie, you've had a baby. Don't sweep the floor. Lay down." The thing was, there weren't any smart people around to tell me that. And the floor needed sweeping. I was the only one who could do it. Bill had his hands full with taking care of the boys and figuring out meals and so on. I could do this. And I did. I was almost finished when Bill came back in with the boys, saw me with the broom, and made me go lie down again.

We went to the doctor. We traveled in the back of an auto rickshaw . . . in the cold wind . . . through the smog. Looking back, most smart people would have told us to take a taxi for the baby's health and our own. The thing was, there weren't any smart people around to tell us that. The baby needed to go to the doctor and we were the ones who could take her. We just did it. She was declared a very healthy girl. Later, we went to the passport office, too.

On Josie's third day, we decided we should try to go to visit our friend who had ridden with us from Kite City into the Big City. Ethan's family lived in the Big City and he'd stayed to have a visit with them. We rented a taxi this time and rode an hour through traffic to get there. Most smart people would have told us not to go visiting into a house full of people and new germs with a three day old baby and a recovering mother. The thing was, there weren't any smart people around to tell us that. We needed to visit and thank our friend. So, we went. Our local friends were astounded that we came to their home, too. It was so fun to surprise them and they were thrilled to see us and so happy with the baby. They passed her around and around, taking pictures of her in everyone's arms. Ethan told us that she was the youngest baby he'd ever held. We were fed tons of delicious food. I learned how to nurse discreetly, in the corner of the bed, while the family members entertained our boys. This family still is so special to us and we visit them every time we come to the Big City.

After about a week, we decided it was time to go home to Kite City. We packed up our apartment, I swept the floor again, and we got into the taxi for the return trip. We made our way back to the house and had to move all our things back in. It was just a few days before Christmas. We wrapped presents, and I made a big meal to remind the boys how special this day was. We tried to keep the house clean. After all, we were supposed to have guests in a few short weeks! God gave us a perfect Christmas: one that probably looked a whole lot more like the first Christmas, anyway.

9

There was a time that I was thankful my kids were crying and screaming in public. After Josie was born, our family was anxiously waiting for our parents to come visit us and meet her. My parents had tickets for mid-January and Bill's parents had tickets for February. We couldn't wait for them to meet our amazing girl, but I was worried because Dad's health had been going downhill and I wasn't sure he'd be up for the trip. I was trying to be optimistic but also realistic at the same time.

Then, we got a call from my Mom. "Honey, your Dad's in the hospital. He's so sick. There's no way we'll make it to India next week. Actually, if you want him to meet Josie, you'd better come home." I tried to remain calm on the phone, but inside, I was already packing with one foot out the door and on the plane. How were we going to do it? We didn't even have Josie's passport yet. How would we get a visa in time? What if we didn't make it? I couldn't travel without her, she was brand new and nursing exclusively. After I hung up the phone, hugged Bill, and cried for a while, we started making plans. Bill called the embassy — several times — telling them not to send the passport to us but to hold it for us at the office so we could come pick it up. We were so worried that they would send it out as we drove there to get it. We also didn't know what it would look like to try to get an exit visa for our newborn. We didn't know how long the process would take. All we knew was we needed to get back as quickly as possible. I looked for one-way flights to America. We packed up our belongings and drove to the Big City.

We spent one rough night in a small hotel room, waking well before our 9 AM appointment at the embassy. Walking in, we said a prayer that the passport would indeed be there. Miraculously, it was still at the office. After about an hour, it was in our hands and we were in another rickshaw going to the visa office. Our flight was for 3:30 AM that night, so we just HAD to get the visa. There was no wiggle room.

As we arrived, I noticed the line stretching around the building and down the sidewalk. It was the line for refugees. It was full of people from another country waiting and hoping for permission to stay. We walked to the much shorter line for people who weren't refugees. It was still fairly long. Bill got a number and we sat down to wait. We were in an outside hall where there were only rows and rows of chairs, mostly filled with refugee people, each with their own numbers. The kids were getting a bit fussy and I was trying to figure out how to feed Josie discreetly while everyone stared at us. James and Carl started running up and down the rows of chairs and I just let them. After about an hour, our number blinked on a big screen. Bill went in only to be told that we needed to fill out the paperwork. What paperwork? The paperwork on the website. What website? He came outside frustrated. He started to tell me that we'd have to take the long rickshaw ride back to the hotel so we could use the internet and print the papers we needed. All of a sudden a man walked up. He told us that we could print the papers at a stand down the road.

We had to laugh as he walked us up to an outdoor cigarette vendor who also happened to have a computer and printer set up. He was making a fortune off the silly foreigners who needed their visa papers. The guy who found us was probably his cousin. Hats off to these entrepreneurial gentlemen. Bill soon had his papers in hand, filled them out, and we all went into the office. I thought the line was outside. Inside the office, there was another line of refugees that went all around the large room. There were also about fifty chairs full of others who were waiting. Bill began to stand in the shorter line again, but the kids were cranky and I was ready to get something done.

I looked around and there, in the corner, was a man at a desk piled high with all sorts of official looking documents. Above his head, in white, block, capital letters was a word: INCHARGE. Well, he was the guy in charge, so I took my three whiny kids and stood directly in front of his desk. He must have been surprised to look up and find this stressed out Mama looking down at him, but he didn't show it. I explained our situation to him. He asked for our papers and took them, putting them directly on a stack that was taken to a back room.

There, I thought, that's just what I was hoping for. We're now on the fast track to getting out of here. My kids were still crying and a wonderful woman sat down and started showing them videos on her iPhone while I nursed Josie. What a gem of a person! Bill was watching the crowd carefully. After about a half hour, he said to me, "Mag, I think you need to take the kids back to the hotel. It's probably going to be awhile. I saw all the other people whose papers went to the back room receive their papers and then leave. Ours haven't come yet so I'm just going to camp out here until they give me our papers."

Well, I wasn't going back to the hotel empty handed. By this time, the nice lady was gone and the boys were whining and crying and Josie was tired. I secured Josie in the sling, grabbed the boys by the hands, and marched back up to Mr. INCHARGE. He seemed surprised to see me. "You don't have your papers yet?" "No."

He got up from his desk, went to the back room, and reappeared with our papers in his hand. He then proceeded to walk Bill around the office, putting our papers at the top of each desk of each official who had to check something, sign, and stamp them. Then, on to the next desk. This happened at least eight times. Finally, they returned our papers and Josie's passport. She had her exit visa. We said a prayer and made our way back to the hotel where we just had to wait for 3:30 AM to roll around. God gave us three cranky children that day. He also gave us favor with Mr. INCHARGE so we could be on our way to see Grandpa!

10

There was a day when I placed a granddaughter in my father's arms. We had gotten through the ordeal of getting her visa to leave the country. We arrived at the airport at midnight, anxiously waiting for our 3:30 AM flight to America. We were going to take a fourteen hour flight and then a two hour flight. Bill was filling the role of baggage man again. He maneuvered our suitcases while I carried and led our exhausted kids. Josie was in the sling where James had been only six short months before. Bill put James on his shoulders while he tried to balance the baggage cart and our carry-ons. Carl followed, half-awake, until his little legs gave out and I began carrying him, too. He was only three and a half. He really didn't understand what was going on. We told him we were going to see Grandma and Papa and that Papa was really sick. He was going to be with Jesus soon. Carl was just happy that he would see his family again.

We settled into our seats for the flight. There were five of us, but we had three seats. James wasn't two yet and we sure wanted to be able to save that $1,000 dollars. The flight attendants had a difficult time trying to figure out how to make sure we all had enough oxygen masks for ourselves, but eventually, they got us situated and we were on our way. James was still too young to sit and watch the movies, but Carl was thrilled when we told him he could watch whatever cartoons he wanted all the way to Grandma's house! We took turns holding Josie and keeping James entertained. Thankfully, he slept a lot, but when he was up, he was UP! He wanted to color, he wanted to walk the aisle, he wanted to play with you, he wanted a snack, he wanted a story, he wanted to listen to music, he wanted to watch a cartoon, he wanted to play a video game . . . and on and on. Bill managed a few hours of sleep on the flight. Between feeding Josie, changing diapers, walking cranky kids up and down the aisle and my restless legs from never having any space to myself, I didn't sleep at all.

I was so excited to see that we were about to land in America. It was about 4:30 local time. We learned that we couldn't get off the plane until 5:00 for some reason. My heart sank. That was the time that all three kids decided that they'd had enough. I had had enough, too. I wanted to call to the captain, "Can't you just open the emergency door and inflate the slide? My kids can do some laps around the plane and everyone would be a whole lot happier!!"

Finally, they opened the doors and we made our way to the line where they were going to let us go in to customs. I have never seen anything like it. Here we were, a few weary Americans and a huge number of weary South Asians. We'd just arrived off a very long flight to a world of lines where rules and regulations needed to be followed. Some of these people had probably never been to the U.S. before. The man who was checking passports made a smashing impression. "Stay behind the line!" He bellowed from his podium at the front. A few sheepish travelers tried to scoot back, but couldn't quite get the balls of their feet behind the line because of the people who were behind them. "I said, STAY BEHIND THE LINE!! Can't you read the sign???!!!" Well, smart man, maybe they can't read the sign. Maybe they're fluent in their own mother tongue . . . Maybe they've been on a crazy long flight and can hardly keep their eyes open to read the sign. We started moving again only to hear another barrage of verbiage from the front. "Get in a line! SINGLE FILE!! Do you know what single file means??!!" Maybe he realized that some of these folks might not know what it meant, so he started again. "One at a time. NO! ONE AT A TIME!" We tried to squeeze ourselves into a tighter line for the drill sergeant at the front. He wasn't satisfied. "I will not let anyone else go through until this is a single file line!" We worked harder. It took about a minute before he was finally satisfied and continued checking passports. Anytime he thought people were getting too pushy or out of order, he'd start the proceedings all over again.

Bill and I looked at each other and groaned. You have got to be kidding us! Here was a guy who was trying, in one instant in one line in one airport to get an entire culture to change their ways. I wanted to explain to him the monumental task he was undertaking. I wanted to chide him for showing these people a hideous example of American culture. I wanted to ask him what had gone so horribly wrong in his day (it was only 5 AM) that he was going to treat an entire airplane of people this way. But, I didn't. I didn't have the capacity. I shuffled along like all the other cattle, dragging my calves with me, got my passport checked and heaved a sigh of relief.

We made our way through all the other lines. Our kids have begun to look at airports as a series of lines we have to get through. I try to set them up for success, but invariably, in those early years, we'd have a complete melt-down in the middle of the airport from at least one, and probably all three, of them. But, we managed to make it to the next flight and into our three seats for the last two hours. At the Chicago airport, we were met by Bill's parents. We were going to borrow their van for our time in the U.S., so we got to hug them before taking off for the hospital. Then, we were off. I remember little about the drive except that I was too excited and anxious to see my father to be tired. All three kids fell asleep.

At the hospital, we took the kids and made our way into the entry. We asked at the reception for my dad's room. She smiled knowingly and gave us the number. We got in the elevator, walked out on the floor and into his room. My mom, sister, niece, and aunt were there. Everyone hushed as I walked across the floor to my Dad. He was so thin I might not have recognized him. He was so weak I couldn't believe these were the same arms that had thrown me in the air and worked for our family and carried us through so much. I laid my baby in those arms. He smiled. A weary, slow, contented, and thankful smile. My heart relaxed and rejoiced at the same time. We made it. He got to hold her. God gave my father another granddaughter.

11

There was a day I watched my father go home. We had been in the U.S. for several weeks. Dad had a bit of a rebound and was able to go home on hospice care. It wasn't a simple life. He had a hospital bed in the main floor of the house. My little sister and niece lived there. We lived there, too. Dad was in a lot of pain, so all the craziness of kids was a bit much. We tried to keep them quiet, but it was hard to do when they were all so little. So, we'd take them visiting or other things to try to give Dad some rest. We even stayed at a friend's house for some of the time so he could have some peace and quiet. There were days he would sit up, eat at the table with us, even want to greet the kids. There were other days he was tired, confused, and quiet. The only church service he ever missed during that time was the one when he was in the hospital. Otherwise, every Sunday Mom would wheel him out to the car and take him to church.

We had Josie's baptism that first Sunday. We wanted Dad to be there. It would be the last family photo I had with him. After a few more weeks, however, Bill and I started talking. How long should we stay? We were supposed to be across the ocean. We had committed to the work and the time we were going to spend. We wanted to be there for Dad, but we didn't want to make things more difficult with the chaos that our young family naturally brought to every situation.

We asked our families, we asked our friends back in Asia, we asked our pastors and mentors. One day, I realized I had never asked Dad. So, on a day when he was more coherent than usual (he was on more morphine than his hospice care nurses had ever seen), I sat down with him. "Dad, I haven't asked you how you feel. We're trying to figure out if we should stay here with you or go back. We want to be here but don't want to make things harder. We want to fulfill our commitment to being there, but also our commitments to you. What do you think?" He turned and looked me straight in the eyes.

"Don't wait around here for me to die. You have to go back. You are needed there. Follow what God told you to do." Well, that was that. Bill and I started making plans to head back across the ocean. I made peace that I wasn't going to see Dad again, that I was going to miss his funeral. We also made plans to spend a little time at our offices in the States so that we could process all these things before going back.

After we had finished that painful packing process, we were ready to leave. I went to hug my family. My Mom and sister clung to me. I walked over to where Dad sat. It was the same chair he had been sitting in when he had told me to go. I hugged him . . . I could hardly speak. "I love you, Daddy."

He hugged me back and then looked straight at me like he had the other day. "You have a Father in Heaven who is a better Daddy than I could ever be. I gave you to him years ago and I continue to trust you to him." Those were the last words my Father ever said to me.

We spent a difficult, but healing, time at our office. We made final preparations and bought our tickets for the return flight. About two days before we were supposed to get on the plane, I got a call from my Mom. "He's going, honey. If you can get here, please come." It was morning. We had already gotten my in-laws' van back to them. We made some calls, cancelled our flight, rented a van, packed our luggage, and rushed down to my hometown, six hours away. We arrived at 5:30 at night. My Dad was lying on his hospital bed. He wasn't responsive, so we sat calmly and waited. Bill had to deliver our rental van to his parents' house and then pick up his parents' van. We played with the kids and talked quietly. My older sister, her husband, and her son arrived. Then, we brought the kids in to say goodbye to Papa. They each came up and hugged him. He opened his eyes, called them all by name, and told them he loved them. That was the last coherent thing he said.

We waited with Mom some more, put the kids to bed, maybe ate something. I don't remember. At around 10:00 that night, Dad started getting very agitated. Mom thought he might need to use the bathroom, so she sent us out of the room. We sisters were chatting when we heard my Mom call, "Come here girls, it's time!"

Dad had his eyes closed, but was rocking side to side on the bed. He kept calling out, "twelve . . . twelve . . . twelve . . ." over and over again. We weren't sure what he was trying to say. Mom kept asking him, "Twelve what? Twelve gates? Twelve disciples?" He said nothing but, "twelve . . . twelve . . . twelve. . ." So, she tried again, "Okay. We've got the message. Twelve. You can stop saying twelve now." We couldn't help but laugh as out of his weak, agitated lips, came, "eleven." My Mom, sisters, and I circled around him, held his hands and each others' as we began to sing. We sang his favorite Easter song "Up from the Grave He Arose", and then, as he left us and arose with His Savior, we sang the "Doxology." Afterwards, we sang one more song, "Amazing Grace." Were there tears? Yes! Was I sad? In that moment I wasn't. I was imagining what that strong, humble, loving, straight-forward, wise, and silly man who had led me all my life was experiencing. I couldn't be anything but happy for him.

When the funeral director arrived, I think he wasn't prepared to find a group of joyful, joking people. We all knew where my Dad was. We all knew that the body in the room was just that: a body. My Father was in his heavenly home. The sickness that had caused tears of pain and sadness to come to our eyes for so many months was now conquered. God gave us rejoicing that night.

12

There was a day when I stood in the middle of the night fanning my baby with a towel. Actually, there were quite a few nights. After we arrived back in Asia from saying goodbye to my Dad, we entered into the single hottest and most miserable time in my life. Now, you may say that it was extra hard because I had just lost my father, I was still trying to transition into this new lifestyle, and I was getting used to having a third child — and all the hormones that go with that! Well, all those things were true, but it really, truly, was stinking hot.

When we arrived back, every day had a high of over 100 degrees. The sun beat mercilessly down on us. The nights didn't cool down. In fact, during one two week stretch, the high was always above 115 and the low never got below 95. Thankfully, we had two window AC units in our bedrooms. They could cool down the house to a manageable 80 degrees if they were running full blast and we kept a curtain across the front room, only trying to cool the bedrooms and kitchen. Unfortunately, the power would cut between eight to twelve hours every day — especially on the hottest days. There just wasn't enough power for all the people trying to use ACs and fans and things. We had a battery inverter that would save up power and run a few lights and fans even when the power was cut. But it turned out that our inverter wasn't working properly. After about 15 minutes with the fan on, the inverter would fail, too. We were left to bake with no moving air. The inside of our house could easily be over 100 degrees, but it wouldn't help to open the windows; it was even hotter outside.

The dust also got worse. With the hot, dry conditions, dust from the construction site behind the house would find its way into every nook and cranny. It would cover the whole house with a layer of dust. Our house helper would come every day and sweep and mop our whole house. By that night, it would be covered again. Our kids would be constantly covered in dust, too, since they spent so much time playing on the floor. There was no way around it. We just worked with it. It was a good thing that we wanted a bath every day, since we were so hot. But, the water that was stored in tanks on the roof would come out piping hot, since the sun was mercilessly beating down on that, too. There was no possible way to take a cool shower.

Also, through the cracks in the doors and windows would come the mosquitoes. We heard many warnings from our local friends as well as health officials about the danger of these mosquitoes. Dengue and malaria were both found in our area. We made sure to have our mosquito nets firmly tied and tucked every night before we went to bed, but there were still welts on our whole family from the hours we were out of our beds. We also purchased some plug-in bug repellers. These would give me headaches if I left them running too long, so I'm sure they had some toxic chemicals in them that I didn't want my family exposed to. But, I didn't want my kids contracting diseases either. . . it was a bit of a conundrum. I thank God that we never had malaria or dengue, but we sure had a lot of itchy days!

The worst time of all was the nighttime, though. We would wash the kids down, put as little clothes as possible on them, tuck in their mosquito nets, and hope the power would stay on. It would come and go through the night. I would be sleeping soundly, with the roar of the AC in my ears, when the power would cut. I would hear the hum of our ceiling fan kick in and pray that the power would come back before the kids woke up. I'd hear the inverter fail (there would be a beeping sound) and the fan would turn off. I'd toss and turn because I was too hot to sleep, and pray. Sometimes, it would come back. A "thank you, Jesus!" would involuntarily explode from my lips. Sometimes, it wouldn't. A "help me, Jesus!" would force itself from my lips as I heard the cries and whines of my kids, too hot to keep sleeping.

I'd untuck my corner of the netting, go to the bathroom, and grab a towel. I'd wet it in the sink and bring it into the kids' room. I'd stand over Josie's bed and start fanning her with the towel. I'd sing to her or make shushing noises as I fanned her. The mosquitoes would find me and start attacking my ankles and the back of my neck. I'd keep fanning. Eventually, she'd quiet down and fall back asleep. If it took awhile, then I'd also have to take turns fanning her brothers who were awakened by her moaning. If or when I got all the kids to sleep, I'd sneak back to my bed and try to fall asleep again. Sometimes, I could, but usually, I couldn't. I was too hot from fanning the kids. So, I would commence praying that the power would come back on so I could sleep. Sometimes, it did. "Thank you, Jesus!" And sometimes it didn't. "Help me, Jesus!" And the kids would wake up and I'd start all over again. This cycle lasted for several months.

The summer really didn't let up until after the monsoon. It was a constant reminder of my weakness. It was a constant reminder of my total reliance on my Savior. God pushed and pulled our family through that summer. He gave us resilience when we didn't even want it anymore.

13

There was a time we rode five people on a motorcycle to the emergency room. As we started our life in Asia, many people voiced their concerns for our safety. They encouraged us to think of our children. They wondered at the corruption or road safety or food and water sanitation or diseases. Through their questions, we heard an unspoken thought, "If you really cared about your kids, you wouldn't go." It was hard to meet these well meaning people with smiles and assurance when we were nervous ourselves. Of course things would be different. Of course we didn't know what we were getting into. But, we had trusted God with our lives and that meant going.

So, we were so thankful to find that we had very few illnesses and accidents to speak of in our new home. We hadn't needed to visit a local doctor except for check-ups when I was pregnant with Josie. We were getting to feel pretty comfortable about our family's health. We were also getting to feel pretty comfortable with our new surroundings. Our family traveled on a motorcycle through the crowded and chaotic streets — all five of us. Carl would ride in front, holding the handlebars with Daddy. Bill would be next. Then James would be stuck between Bill and I. I'd usually try to keep one arm around him and one leg over his leg because he liked to fall asleep while we drove. Josie would be strapped to my hip in the baby sling and I had to ride side-saddle because it was inappropriate for any woman to ride with her legs spread apart over the seat. We'd go for drives on a Sunday afternoon. We'd go to the grocery store. We'd visit friends. We even took an hour's drive out to a bird sanctuary outside of town. So, it seemed like nothing at all to pack the family onto the bike and head to Coffee Cafe for a treat one afternoon.

Coffee Cafe was the cheaper, South-Asianer version of Starbucks that had opened in our city. We could get coffee drinks — as long as we liked them super-sweet — or slushies for the kids. We arrived, ordered drinks, and sat at a little glass table with comfy chairs around it. James was as energetic as always and we usually had our biggest challenge just getting him to sit down and relax. But, in Kite City, people were much more forgiving about loud or rambunctious children -- especially if they had James's blonde hair and blue eyes. Our drinks arrived and the kids were so excited about their blue slush drink they were sharing. They took turns slurping through the straw until James had enough sugar in his system to get him up and moving again. I was just telling him to calm down and sit down, for the hundredth time, when CRASH! He whacked his drink over with his hand, spilling the slush and breaking the glass it was in. The waiter came over to see what happened and offered to make the kids another one. I was trying to clean up the broken glass and blot the slush from the front of my shirt when I heard another crash. James had run around the table, slipped on spilled slush, and landed with the side of his head on the edge of the glass coffee table. We looked at his ear lobe — it was sliced clean through. AAAGGGHHH!!!!

I grabbed a sterile wet wipe from my bag (a must for our lifestyle), took James by the ear, and pinched it to stop the bleeding. Josie was still on my hip in the sling and James was on my lap crying. Bill asked where a hospital was and we rushed down the stairs, threw the kids on the bike, and I rode straddling the seat because this was not a time for propriety.

A few blocks away we found the hospital. It was a small building with the entrance tucked back in a side street. We walked in and made our way through the crowd of people with our crying kids. There was a desk in the back of the receiving room where Bill went to sign us in. We sat in the waiting area while the doctor was busy with someone else. As we waited, a woman with a large wound on her leg was wheeled on a gurney and parked right in front of us. Bill took James to see the doctor and Carl amused himself by watching some fish in a dirty fish tank in the corner. Every person in the place was staring at the strange foreign folks. Bill came back to tell me that the doctor said he needed to put in a few stitches. He handed James to me so that he could walk to the pharmacy by the entrance and buy the things the doctor said he needed -- sutures, gloves, antiseptic, etc. After that, he held James and followed a nurse up some stairs to an operating room. I could hear James's screams from the waiting area. After a while, I didn't hear anything anymore. I started to look around while Carl kept watching fish. I was so thankful for the fish! I looked down in the empty seat next to me and there was a used syringe -- without a cap on the needle -- lying in the crease of the seat. Boy was I glad I hadn't sat in that seat! I picked up the syringe and held it up to the man at the desk, "I found this in the seat here."

"Oh, okay," he said nonchalantly, and dropped it into the trash can beside his desk. I shuddered involuntarily and looked up to see Bill walking down the stairs, carrying James's limp body. I rushed up to him.

"What happened?" I asked. "They wouldn't let me come into the room with them. They put him under. For three stitches. We need to get out of here before I start flipping tables." We paid our bill quickly and headed out the door. I had quite a ride back to the house, trying to balance a passed-out James and a baby while we bumped over the rough road to our home. We got up into the flat and just held our boy while Carl and Josie started to play around us. He was still completely unresponsive so we prayed that everything would be okay and that he'd come out of the anesthesia without any problems.

Eventually, he started to come around. He kicked his legs and yelled. I held him and tried to calm him and told him that he was with us again and everything was okay. He calmed down and tried to open his eyes. We asked him if he'd like a treat, since his Coffee Cafe experience was cut short. He wanted a coke float. I wasn't ready to let go of our boy, so Bill went and bought some coke and ice cream. He made them for all of us and I turned on a movie to watch. As James took his first sips and bites, he looked at me sleepily, "Mama, the ice cream's going right to my ear and making me all better." Oh, how I loved our boy. Oh, how thankful I was to see him awake and happy. Oh, how frustrated I was just a few days later when he pulled out all the stitches by himself. Still, in the middle of the chaos, his ear was fine. There was no infection. He still has that scar on his ear and loves to show people. God brought us to a place that could treat our son and reminded us of the things that were not in our power.

14

There was a time I sang Celine Dion in a village. We were having a much-needed vacation. It had been a very trying summer — the hottest and most miserable that I could have imagined. We packed the kids and our bags and took a trip to the mountains. We spent time on a houseboat and at a little guest house in a village. There were cool breezes, tasty foods, friendly neighbors, and rest. We even got to spend some time with a couple we'd met before. They lived in those mountains and showed us around a bit. We enjoyed ourselves thoroughly.

Our favorite part was when we were up in the village guest house. Of course, we stood out in this village, just as we always do. Josie was about eight months old, standing on her own, and smiling at everything that moved. I was dressed like a local. I think this added to our ability to connect with everyone we met. Several times during our stay, I was walking to a small shop in town to buy something and I was invited into a home for tea. I think most of them were just wanting a better look at Josie. One home had three young women in it (one young wife and two sisters). They loved talking with me and I with them. They asked me all about America and I asked them about their families. We shared tea together twice.

I was admiring their beautiful, embroidered clothes one day when they asked me about my outfit. A common question is, "How much did it cost?" I have a hard time with that question, coming from the west, and I felt ashamed because I actually bought it in the U.S. at a shop and paid way too much for it. It would have been half that price if I had gotten it on the other side of the world. After sheepishly telling them the amount, they smiled. The young wife asked me, "Would you trade? I have a new suit that cost the same upstairs. Would you trade with me?" Well, I could imagine that a suit of clothes like they were wearing, with hand embroidered flowers all over it, would be quite lovely. I was wanting a suit like that for the winter months and figured if it cost that much, it would be worth it. I went with them upstairs and they pulled a suit out of a wooden chest in the corner. "Here, try it on!" All of them smiling with anticipation. My new friend was already starting to change her clothes so she could try on mine! Well, I was in the excitement of the moment, but as I reached for the suit, I saw, not the soft colors and delicate threaded embroidery I was expecting, but a fake satin suit in hot pink and purple. It had gaudy gold and silver lacy flowers tacked on it and sequins and jewels. In a word — Woah!

Now, since I moved to South Asia, my tolerance, and even preference, for bright and shiny increased by 2000%. But this suit was even past what I was able to appreciate. Still, here I was standing in front of a new friend who was already waiting to try on my suit! So, I changed out of mine and put on hers. It was a little big, but fit okay. The girls started exclaiming about how nice I looked in it. They wanted to show their mother, so we walked downstairs. At this point, I realized I was never getting my clothes back. I had forgotten the all-important phrase, "I will have to talk to my husband first." This phrase works in almost every situation. Also, I'm not sentimental about stuff. I chalked it up to a learning experience, reminded myself that I had a few other changes of clothes in my bag back at the guest house, and walked down the steps. The rest of the family exclaimed about how nice we both looked in our traded suits. Then, we sat down for more tea.

The girls started asking me about American movies and songs. "Do you know Titanic?" Yes, I had seen it. They started humming the melody for "My Heart Will Go On." "Do you know that song?" Yes, I did. "Will you sing it for us?" Hmmm. Now, normally, I'm not too excited to sing Celine Dion. First of all, it's not my style. Second, she can sing her songs just great without me. But, here was this whole room of family asking for it. So, I told them I'd sing for them only if they would sing for me. They obliged and then it was my turn. How wide their eyes got as I began. "You know the whole thing! She knows the whole thing," they whispered. I didn't remember the whole thing, but it felt good to have my efforts appreciated. "Just like the recording," their elderly grandfather commented. Well, not quite!

After sharing songs, I took Josie from the adoring Aunties and made my way back to the guesthouse. I felt pretty conspicuous since this style of dress was usually reserved for wedding parties, but I was hopeful that I could make my way back to the room and change easily enough. Bill greeted me at the gate, staring at the shimmering, sparkling splendor, "Um, what happened to your clothes?" Turns out, the suit I had just traded was his favorite one I owned. I had traded it for that shining extravaganza. I apologized, changed, and we continued to have a wonderful vacation. When we returned home, I gave the suit to my house helper — a young woman who would have been thrilled to wear it to the next family wedding. I made sure, from then on, to know which clothes were Bill's favorite and to keep the husband excuse ready at all times. God was going to give me a chance to have many of the beautiful embroidered suits I had admired on those young women. He was going to move us to those mountains. But not yet.

15

There was a time I spent three days making green bean casserole. The group of expats we spent time with in Kite City were going to celebrate Thanksgiving. It was our second Thanksgiving overseas and Josie was almost one year old. I honestly don't remember much of our first Thanksgiving in the country. I was eight and a half months pregnant and a bit preoccupied. But this year, we were going to celebrate in style. Each family was bringing something special to the table. I was in charge of green bean casserole, cornbread casserole, collard greens, and pumpkin pie.

Green bean casserole: my ultimate favorite Thanksgiving food!!! Seriously, I'd eat a truckload of the stuff! So, how do you make it without cans of cream of mushroom soup or little fried onions from a pop-top lid? What's a girl to do? I almost feel silly writing about this stuff. Did you know that my Grandmas didn't have any of that when they made their Thanksgiving meals? Or any meals when they were younger? So what have I to complain about? That's the pep-talk I gave myself as I looked up recipes on the internet (that, of course, my Grandmas never had) and got down to business. Here was the plan:

Day One: Buy whole pumpkin, several kilos of green beans, mushrooms, onions, greens, and other supplies. Bring them all home and process them. I washed the outside of the pumpkin and put it in the pressure cooker to steam. I soaked the beans in vinegar water, cut them, and boiled them in bullion. I soaked the greens, rinsed, and chopped them. I fried them in bullion-flavored butter with onions and other spices and put them in the fridge to be reheated for the celebration.

Day Two: Make pumpkin pie filling. Make mushroom soup mix. Make fried onions. I mixed pumpkin pie filling with eggs, sugar, pumpkin, spices that I had ground myself, etc. I put that in the fridge. I chopped the mushrooms and onions, creamed them into a soup mix, and combined them with the boiled beans from the day before. I put that in the fridge. I heated oil, sliced some more onions, coated them in flour and spices, and deep fried them. I saved them in paper towels for the next day.

Day Three: Here's where it all came together. I was feeling great because I'd gotten so much done beforehand. I felt like everything was in place. I took out my pie pan, pastry cutter, and rolling pin (that my Mom gave me while I was home). I cut the delicious butter into the white flour — a delicacy at our house. I laid the pie crust into the pan, grabbed the pumpkin filling, blended it together, poured it into the pan and slid it into my convection oven. I said a quick prayer that the power would stay on long enough to bake my pie. Ten minutes later, I found out that this was one of those opportunities to learn patience and flexibility. The power went out.

Oh, Dear God, give me strength! I could just see my pie sitting there, wasting away in the oven, for two hours. In the meantime, I had to get the casserole put together so that if the power came back, I could still get everything baked. Thankfully, I'd already cooked everything in the casserole. It just needed to be warmed, but at this point, I wasn't quite sure if I'd make it. I still had to make a cornbread casserole. I pulled out my precious canned goods from my bin. I had the corn and the box of cornbread mix, delivered from America, ready to go. I mixed everything together and set it aside. My convection oven had barely enough room for one casserole dish in it. I realized that there was no way everything would be cooked through.

The power came back on and my pie started baking again. By this time, I needed to start getting kids bathed and looking half-way decent. I forgot that if I put them in their tops with white cotton pants early, their knees would be filthy from playing on the floor by the time we walked out the door. I remembered as I pulled the pie out of the oven and saw them happily crawling around with dust-covered clothes.

One more thing I'd forgotten: my oven didn't cook evenly. One side of my pie crust was burnt. Well, what can you do? I put in the cornbread casserole and hoped for the best. It took twice as long to cook as would be normal because the voltage coming into the house was low that day. So, I waited and waited and finally took it out even though it was still a little bit crunchy. Then, in went the green bean casserole. I prayed that it would cook in the half hour we had left before we left. I heated the greens on the stove and wrapped everything else up in towels and put them in a large carry bag. After twenty minutes, the power went out again. Oh, well.

So, then we just had to go a few blocks to our foreign friend's house. We hopped on the motorcycle. I balanced Josie and the bag of food. I decided that the food was hot enough because it was burning red marks into my thighs as we bumped over the biggest pot holes in the whole city. As we rode, I decided it was only fitting to write a new version of the classic Thanksgiving song, "Over the

River and Through the Woods" to commemorate this new holiday experience. Here it is:

Over the potholes and through the poo
To our neighbor's house we go.
The bike is upright, it's just turning night
We've got to keep it slow.
Over the speed bumps, around the cows
Mosquitoes up your nose
But who gives a care if we all get there
As over the potholes we go.

The evening was great! We ate and ate and ate and everything really tasted a lot like home. We even somehow found time to chat and hang out around the nine kids — yes nine! — eight years old and under. It was so fun to swap stories and make new memories with the people who had truly become family as we shared a new life together. God gave us a Thanksgiving that was truly thankful.

16

There was a time I thought my kid fell off a roof. I had been excited about going to weddings ever since I knew we were moving to South Asia. I'd seen the videos of weddings -- brides decked out in henna, colorful saris, lots of food, lots of dancing, lots of people. Seemed like the kind of event I could really let loose in.

But, when we got the invitation, I was pretty apprehensive. First of all, I was not going by myself or with my husband, but with my husband and my one, three, and four year olds. The aforementioned selfie-ambush was high on my mind. There was also the realization that this would be a Muslim wedding. In this neighborhood, that meant no dancing, no music, and no mingling of the sexes at all. Finally, it was in the slum area where some of our best friends lived. We weren't sure what to expect, but wanted to make sure that we were a blessing and not an embarrassment to these friends of ours who had invited us. We also deliberated and deliberated about what to give as a gift until the father of the bride asked us specifically. Would we supply the food for the wedding? So, it was decided. We were ordering spicy rice with meat to feed 300 people!

The day came and I wrestled my boys into their traditional dress. They hated wearing local clothes, but I insisted that it was what kids at these events should wear. I worked on our hair, clothes, bangles, earrings, sandals, and then we were finally ready. We walked to their home and were immediately separated. Bill was taken to the men's area of the tent while I was directed to the bamboo, tin, and tarp home of our hosts. They sat the kids and I down on the bed and I was surrounded with family members and friends. I was told that they were getting the bride ready in the back room. There were suitcases open and they were rummaging through them to find all the things that she would need to be dressed as a bride for this day. I was sitting with the kids, trying to help them drink the cups of chai and eat the snacks that were brought for us while I was pummeled with questions and comments from so many people -- only understanding about 25% of what was said.

About this time, Carl knocked the tea onto my brand new blue dress. It gave me second degree burns on my leg. At least it didn't land on Josie. James started crying and complaining that he didn't want to be there, so one of the ladies offered to take him to be with his Dad. Josie was hungry, and as she whined, all the Aunties started trying to give her every candy or cookie they could find. Then, they told us that the food was ready and we should go to the tent. When we were walking to the women and kids side of the tent, I tried to peek into the men's side to see how Bill was faring, but I didn't see him or James anywhere.

They brought plates of food that I found delicious, but Carl found too spicy. He started complaining, so everyone came to find out what was wrong. How do you tell them that he doesn't like the food? They were all trying to make him feel better by talking and playing with him -- which only made him feel worse. Someone else offered to take Carl to be with Bill, but he just cried louder that he didn't want to leave me. Then Josie started crying because she was in need of a nap. As I was trying to get her to lie on my shoulder for a rest, a woman came running into the tent. "The little boy is going to die!!! He's falling from the roof!"

She motioned to me to follow her, and I grabbed Jo, took Carl by the hand, and ran outside, terrified that I was going to find James in pieces at the bottom of the unfinished apartment building in the neighborhood. Instead, I saw about 200 people from the community looking up, pointing and screaming. There was James' head. It was lodged into the brick railing surrounding the roof where, apparently, they had taken Bill to eat his dinner since he was the most prestigious guest. God bless James's curiosity and his protruding ears! He had tried to get a better view of everything and had gotten himself stuck. His little eyes were searching that hysterical crowd of brown faces and then latched onto my peach one. I smiled up at him and tried to yell that he would be fine and everything would be okay. I'm sure he couldn't hear anything I was saying through all the doomsday screaming coming from my neighbors. About this time I saw a young man start to scale the building from the outside, climbing from unfinished window to unfinished balcony. He was up three stories and trying to grab James's head and shove it back through the hole, moving it up and down the opening to find the place it would go through.

I heard later from Bill that he was in the middle of his dinner, eating with his hand of course, when he heard James crying. He turned around and saw what was going on, but couldn't get at him with the plate on his lap. He was trying to find a way to clean his hand off when a man up on the roof went for a hammer. He was about to start breaking down the wall when Bill jumped in to reassure James and gingerly guide his head to the wider part of the railing and then out. As James will tell you, "I only got a little scrape right here!" as he points to the back of one ear.

Well, I then and there resigned to not being a blessing to the event and settled for being the entertainment. I couldn't leave yet, since the bride hadn't come out, but I used the excuse that I was worried about my son to spend the rest of the wedding standing out in the road area with Bill, the kids, and a bunch of other wedding goers. The kids played in the dirt and completely wrecked their brand new traditional clothes. I also got a chance to look around and see that most of the other boys were in button-downs and jeans. So much for being contextual!

We watched the families go through the dowry items that the bride's family was giving to the groom's family. They wrote down how much everything was worth so they could sign it and agree that it was correct. Then the groom arrived and all the female relatives gathered around and sang chants while they put garlands of money around his neck. The kids started throwing stones at each other and I had to separate them.

The family loaded the dowry into a waiting truck, packed up the groom, and then we got to see the bride. The fancy, sparkly dress and jewelry that I had seen in the house was completely covered in a black robe. We couldn't see her face, but we could hear her crying. She and her relatives were wailing. This is how I learned that a wedding in this country is more sad for the bride than happy. She leaves her home and her family and is forever considered as part of her husband's family more than her own from that day on. I got to hug this girl and pray over her as they put her into the car to drive away from her home forever. Maybe I was able to be a blessing after all. The kids started wrestling in the dirt and Josie's diaper started to smell. We said our goodbyes and made for home. God protected James and delivered us safely from our first Asian wedding.

17

There was a time a farmer's wife crossed the ocean. The first time I welcomed my Mom into my South Asian home was a beautiful day. This was planned. We knew that the summer would be exceedingly too hot for her and the winter would be uncomfortably cold, so we picked one of the only two comfortable months in our area -- it had to be November or February. She came in February, arriving in the middle of the night to the Big City. She had never been out of the country, never crossed the ocean, never entered an international airport, and here she was landing after midnight in one of the biggest cities in the world. I wanted so badly to be the one to meet my Mom at the airport, but Bill was adamant that he would go because he didn't want my Mom and I taking public transportation in the middle of the night. I had to bow to his wisdom and protective instincts. He saw her starting to walk out of the airport with her luggage and, after hugging him, she asked him, "Where was I supposed to get my stamp?"

Well, it turns out that a sixtyish-year-old woman who is traveling alone in a foreign country doesn't get questioned very often. I guess people must assume that she knows what she's doing, because what woman in her right mind would travel to a brand new country all by herself at that age unless she is experienced? The answer: my mother. She had just walked right past the immigration desks and on to pick up her luggage and no one had stopped her. No one had asked her anything. She was about to leave the airport without an entry stamp. Thankfully, they realized this soon enough and Bill talked to the security guards who brought her back to the sheepish immigration agents who processed her passport and sent her on her way. What a way to start your experience!

The next day, we took her to a couple places we knew when we had lived in the city. She rode in the back of an autorickshaw with our family — six of us on a bench that comfortably fit two adults. She walked through the crowded streets and ate at a table restaurant where she cringed a bit as they wiped off the plate she was about to eat on with a filthy rag. The next day, we took her on the metro -- in the common car -- during rush hour. Afterwards, she was saying how sorry she was feeling that she was so smushed onto a short young woman that she couldn't give her any room and couldn't get her feet under her to stop leaning on her. Bill assured her that the woman was much happier to have Mom smushing her than some random guy. That made Mom feel better.

We took Mom to some tourist stops. She got to see majestic, ancient buildings. She also got to see our reality of being celebrities wherever we went. It helped the process to have two Mama Bears protecting the kids from selfie-seekers. We rode out to our home city through the villages and on all the bumpy roads. Mom's constant attitude never wavered — even as we swerved past busses and bullock carts, stray dogs and school kids — "I figure they know what they're doing and I just have to hold on."

In our city, she rode side-saddle on the back of our motorcycle as Bill drove her around for a tour. She rode with the kids and I on the back of a bicycle rickshaw to visit friends or get groceries. We went to the slum area where she drank tea and smiled. We had snacks and soda with a caretaker of a local historical site in his home. She found ways to play with the kids in our little apartment and never complained about the accommodations or trying to figure out a squatty potty if the need arose.

She also adventured into cooking with me. She tried local dishes. She shopped with me and helped me cook. She even brought along everything she needed to make one of my all-time favorites: turtle cake. We coaxed my convection oven into baking it for us and I savored every mouthful -- as much for her sacrifice as for the flavor.

I was amazed. I was floored. Here was this woman who had never asked to see the world, who had never imagined crossing an ocean, but who was ready for all of the goofiest adventures we threw at her because we were there. She got it. She knew this was our life and she wanted to truly experience the life we were living. "I just want to do what you normally do. I'm along for the ride," she would say. We didn't feel the need to apologize for our life there or try to soften it much (except for having her come in February instead of June). God's grace shone through my Mother's willingness to just be there. She wanted to see what we saw and understand what we understood. She wanted to be a blessing rather than expecting us to bless her and accommodate for her. There was no better way for a person to be a part of our lives there. It changed her, too. When she could see what it was we were talking about, she understood at a level that none of our other family or friends could. She could empathize when we'd talk of a struggle. She could rejoice when we talked of a triumph. It was beyond our expectation of her visit, but it wasn't beyond God's. God gave us this visit at time we were really needing family.

18

There was a time we learned we were losing our community. Our trip to the mountains had truly been a refreshing one for us. It was such a beautiful, green, cool place with space for my kids to run and time for us to relax. It brought us so much renewal. But, it also brought us a surprise. We had agreed to move to Kite City partly because we knew there would be a few other foreign families in the area. They were believers, too. We could get together and pray, sing, and read the Word. We could encourage each other in this new place, share what we'd learned about the culture, help each other when things were difficult, and be a kind of family for each other as we navigated this new life. It was truly a blessing to have them close by. But while we were in the mountains, we heard from other people that the family who had lived first in Kite City was starting a new job. At that time, we didn't know they were even considering it. We had agreed to be together in Kite City for two years and after that, who knew. This was our plan and we'd only been in the area for about a year so far.

So, when we heard the news, we didn't know what this new job would mean for our friends, but we began wondering if they were staying in Kite City. It didn't take long to find out that our friends were, indeed, going to move — and in a matter of a few months. This led to discussions with the rest of our friends. Everyone was moving to new places. These foreign friends of ours would all be leaving Kite City before we'd lived there for one and a half years. Bill and I didn't know what to do. We didn't want to leave our new life in Kite City just as we were starting to get used to it, but we also didn't want to be there without other foreigners or believers. We started to pray.

In fact, Bill spent at least three hours a day shut up in his 'office.' It was really a small storage closet that he had put a desk, a lamp, and a fan into. He would close and lock that door so that he could have a small sanctuary against the craziness of three small kids living in a marble-floored flat. He was praying for some kind of direction, some kind of leading. What should we do? Where should we go? What in the heck was God doing?

Within these few months, we started to say our goodbyes. First one family, then, another friend, then another family left. There were lots of hugs, lots of packing, and lots of goodbyes. We didn't know when or how we would run into these people again. They had become our support system, our friends, and our family in such a short time. They were the only ones who truly knew what it was like to live as a foreigner in Kite City. They knew us and we knew them. It was a hard time to watch them all move on while we stayed.

We kept praying. Finally, we met a friend of a friend of a friend. Through a series of answered prayers, we found our answer. We would move in a few short weeks to the mountains to work with a company up there. We would have another community of foreigners to spend time with. It was hard to believe that God was sending us to the very place we had gone to find refreshment and relaxation. I was floored. I often say that God sent us to Kite City for many reasons, but one of the biggest ones was so that we would know the blessings of the new home he would send us to. We would have never known the blessing of having a yard for our children to play in. We would have never known the blessings of having natural beauty all around us. We would have never known the blessing of the much more moderate climate. We would have never known that our new city was relatively clean, relatively uncrowded, relatively beautiful. The mountains had their own set of challenges and we were going to see many of them first-hand. But, God also gave us the chance to see the blessings He had prepared for us.

19

There was a time when our neighbors squabbled over our Christmas tree. We were leaving Kite City. We were moving to the mountains. It was a bittersweet time for us. We were looking forward to what God was doing with this move, but we were sad to say goodbye to our few local friends in the area. We were friends with Nada. We were friends with our house helper and Bill's new language helper's families in the slum area. Besides that, we didn't have many friends.

When we had moved in, we were eyed with suspicion by our neighbors. We heard reports that some people were saying that we were with the CIA. Haha! Yes, most CIA operatives move into an unknown, small city with their pregnant wife and two small children! Anyway, others were sure that we drank alcohol and ate pork in our house — things that would make us unclean. This seemed true to the fact that, when neighbor women came to meet Josie, they wouldn't even drink the water that we offered them. This is seen as an offense in this culture, but the only thing we could imagine is they thought we were an unclean family. So, when it was time for us to pack up and move, we were surprised that several families came to see us before we left — families that had never paid us a visit or invited us into their own homes.

We were surprised until they started asking us what we were going to do with our furniture, our fridge, our AC units, our . . . well, you get the idea. All of our neighbors were hoping they could cash in on our move by buying our things at a very cheap price. When we moved in, we paid high prices for the things in our home. Everyone knew that we didn't know what fair prices were, so everyone charged us way too much. When some of our friends found out how much we paid for certain things, they would shake their heads, "You got cheated!" Well, we knew that, and we told them so, but what were we to do? We didn't have the language or the knowledge to challenge these things. And, what do you do when it is 100 degrees outside and you need a fridge? You pay what you must. Our friends couldn't argue with that.

Here we were on the way out and, again, people were hoping to cheat us. One family from upstairs, whom I had actually spent a little time with, came to ask for several items. We sold them a few things, but said that we couldn't sell everything until we had thought it all through. Then, the husband asked, "Could you sell us your Christmas tree?" I almost laughed aloud. Our Christmas tree?

It was a half-dried up, spindly, sad little house plant with lights and decorations still hanging from it. The only reason that it looked green anymore was because the lights were green in color (the only lights we could find in the bazaar that first Christmas.) I smiled politely and told him that he could have the tree for free as a gift. We'd paid less than $5 for the tree, so we didn't care. We wouldn't be able to move it up to the mountains anyway.

Later, after I had taken off the decorations and packed them away and brought the tree up to his flat, I wondered if they had wanted the tree with all the decorations on it. Well, he hadn't asked for that and Christmas decorations were hard to come by in the land where no one but us celebrated Christmas. So, maybe he was disappointed. I'll never know.

The very next day, Nada and I were talking on the phone. I told her I was worried people would start being our friends now just because they wanted something from us. I knew this could happen and I was trying not to let my heart go hard. She told me that she really didn't care if she got anything of ours — except our Christmas tree. "I just really like your tree. Can I have it when you leave?" Oh no! I wanted to laugh again . . . or cry! I told her, very apologetically, that I had just given the tree to her relative who lived down the hall. "Oh, that's okay. Don't worry about it." I told her she could find the exact same kind of tree for less than $5 just down the road at the plant nursery. I knew she had the money to buy one if she wanted it. I visited her home a year later. She didn't have the tree. It must have been something special about ours. Maybe it was the decorations.

There was another neighbor who asked about our tree, too. I never will know exactly why all these neighbors wanted our tree. Maybe it was just something to remember us by?? Probably not. Anyway, after a few more thinly veiled visits from neighbors who were wanting to make some money off us, we negotiated a deal with our landlord. He wanted to rent out our flat as a furnished flat. So, we sold him everything in a package deal. We might have made less than if we had portioned off our things to different buyers, but we sure saved ourselves a lot of headache and hurt feelings. It was perfectly acceptable in this culture to give the excuse that we were beholden to our landlord and must give him first dibs on all our things.

Still, there were the matter of so many small things that we couldn't fit in our ten bags we would ship to the mountains. 500 pounds of luggage. 500 pounds of our whole life wrapped in packing tape. We couldn't fit in lots of miscellaneous kitchen goods, clothes, toys, household items, etc. So, we decided that we would use them to bless our friends in the slum area. We alternated giving bags to our house helper and language helpers. On one of these days, when I was sending home a bag with my house helper, a beautiful girl of fifteen years, I told her, "Have you ever been able to give anything to someone who has less than you?" She looked at me shyly, and a bit confused, and shook her head. She didn't know many people who had less than her. She shared a makeshift home with her extended family. She had to work sweeping and cleaning three houses to try to make ends meet. She had needed to quit school at the age of twelve so she could do this. How was she ever able to give to others? I continued, "In these weeks, our family has given many things to your family. We know that you can use many of these things for yourselves. But, maybe there are things that you can't use or don't need. Now, you have more than your neighbors. You can share some of the things with them. You can be the one who is generous."

Her eyes shone and she smiled so big. Again, I told her, "There have been times when our family has had very little. Others have shared with us. Now we have more, so we can share with you. Now you have more, so it is your turn to share. God blesses us so that we can bless others. Will you try to bless others with some of what I've given you?" She smiled again. Then, her eyes teared up and her face became downcast. "If my father will let me, I will give." I realized. There were no decisions in her life that were left up to her. She wasn't able to judge if it was right to give away anything she was given. That right was left up to her father. Then her eyes brightened again, "I will talk to him. I will try." She clutched the bag and hurried home. I still don't know what happened with those things, but I was encouraged by her desire to share.

In the midst of the craziness and selfishness of our relatively wealthy neighbors trying to get for themselves, here was a young woman with practically nothing who wanted to be generous. God gave me a glimpse of a generous heart to remember in Kite City.

Lake City

As we flew into our new city, we could see the snow-capped peaks that surrounded us, the green fields in the valley, the slanted roofs of the houses, the completely different atmosphere that was to be our new home. I was as excited about this new prospect as I was when we left for Kite City from the Big City. There were so many new things to experience, so many things that seemed to me easier than in our old home. I thought, "Finally, we will start to have a normal life here. Finally, the trials we have been facing will smooth out and we will be able to really move forward." I figured that everything that we had experienced was the pruning stage, the preparing stage. In my mind, we had passed our tests and were now ready for a simpler, more comfortable life. In some ways, it was true. The climate, our home, the beauty around us, and even the culture were different and easier for us. We were also going to have some foreign families around us. Again, it was God's grace that we didn't know the new trials that awaited us. We were able to be thankful for the blessings and not worry about the struggles that were still to come.

1

There was a time when my neighbor picked lice from my hair. I grew up on a farm. I had seen lice, but never had them. There wasn't anything more creepy-crawly to me than when we had lice checks in school. The teacher would take out a fine-toothed comb and run it between the layers behind our necks and ears. All of us would start itching just thinking about it. Yuck! But, I'd never actually had them . . . until we visited the shepherds.

When we moved to the mountains, we found a beautiful house with a big yard and garden and a caretaker family that lived next door. Our backyard was a cricket field, but not just that. Every spring and fall, families of migratory shepherds would come through on their way to the summer and winter pastures. For several weeks, we would have a neighborhood of chickens and goats and horses and about five to ten tents staked behind our house. I wanted to meet these ladies and get to know them better, so I would walk around to the entrance of the field and go visiting with the kids. They would welcome us into their tents and we'd sit down on woolen mats as they busied themselves with making us tea and flatbread. We'd try to chat, since their language was a bit different than the one that I'd learned, and find that we could figure out quite a lot to say to one another. The kids would sometimes run around with the shepherd kids or come into the tent and lie down on the blankets next to me. This is, I think, where the problem arose.

Shepherds live with animals. Animals who aren't treated tend to have lice. So, my kids rolled around, picked up nits, and that was that. I can remember after that week that I felt like the dandruff on my head was getting a lot more itchy. I commented to Bill that I thought we'd better find some better shampoo or something. It never occurred to me to check my head.

Then, one morning, as I combed out Josie's hair after her bath, I saw it! A louse! AAAHHHHGGGHHHH!!!! There was nothing that could have prepared me for that discovery. I promptly cried. Then, I checked her head completely. Lots of nits. Then I checked the boys' heads. They had nits, too. So did Bill. Then, he checked my hair. I had them, too!! How was I going to get rid of lice in this place? I didn't know the first thing about what to do except that these things HAD to go!

First things first, I buzzed the boys' hair. Next came Bill's hair. I buzzed his, too. Frankly, I wanted to buzz Josie's and my hair as well but just couldn't do it. I sent Bill down to the pharmacy to see what he could find. While he was gone, I stripped all the beds and started a mammoth job of washing everything in antiseptic soap and drying it in the sun. This took about 4 days to get through everything. As I put the first load of wash in the machine, Bill came back with a little bottle of shampoo that said it killed lice. It didn't kill the nits, though, so that meant I was going to have to fine-comb all of our hair for two weeks until we got rid of every single nit.

I had a routine. At bath time, we would wash one kid. After he was clean, I'd sit with him on a beanbag (I figured they were easier to clean) and fine-comb the hair. After I continued that process with the other two kids, it was Bill's turn. Then me. My hair was long and the hardest to work on. One warm day, towards the beginning of this ordeal, Bill took me out on the front porch so he could see better. He was working on my hair when my neighbor, Amy, came up. I had already told her about the lice and she understood. She'd seen me visiting the shepherds.

"Here, Sister, let me do that for you," she interrupted.

"Oh, no," I insisted, "this work is much too dirty for me to ask you to do it." I felt so ashamed that our family was having to go through this. Also, I didn't want to inconvenience her.

She looked at Bill, with my hair all tangled in his fingers and around the comb trying to figure out what to do next. She laughed, "He is a man. He doesn't know how to do it. Let me do it for you."

I argued again, "No, really, I don't want to trouble you. We can manage."

She got serious, "Your mother and your sisters are far away. I am your sister now. This is work for a sister to do. Let me do this because we are family."

My eyes filled with tears. I couldn't disagree again. God had put me in this home where I had a sister who would stoop to comb nits out of my hair. She did this for several more days until all the nits were gone. I never imagined that I would have family like this on the other side of the world. I never imagined that I would find this family because of getting lice in my hair. That wasn't my idea of a good way to go about it. Yet, I sure saw what true family looked like during those days of sitting on the porch as Amy cleaned my hair.

After that experience, I had someone bring me some of the heavy-duty lice shampoo from the States. I didn't have to stop visiting my backyard neighbors. We just started coming home and showering right after any visit to their homes. God gave us a lice-free home, but more importantly, God gave me a sister right next door.

2

There was a day I sang the Lord's Prayer for a group of women who had just lost everything. I had traveled to the Big City. My friend, Gabriella, was coming for a visit. Bill encouraged me to go to the Big City to meet her, do some sight-seeing, and then bring her back to our house. This was a fun idea since I almost never had time alone with my friends in our new life. So I excitedly left for the Big City.

The day I left, we had to take an alternate route to the airport because it had rained a lot and some of the major roads were flooded. Still, I made it out of the city and had a wonderful time with my friend. After a day or two, my phone wouldn't work to call Bill and the kids. I figured that somehow the water had wrecked communication. This wasn't the first time things like this had happened and cell service was always sketchy, so I just figured I'd connect with him when I got back.

The morning we were arriving back, I had tried to look at the paper and internet to see how the situation was in our town. Was the flooding bad? Would we be able to make it back okay? There wasn't really any information. I asked at the ticket counter at the airport. They told me that planes were still coming and going, so we would be able to get into the city. We had planned to hire a taxi from the airport back to my house. I figured they would know alternate routes to bring us home if the main roads were still flooded and worst case scenario, if it was really bad, we could probably hire a boat to take us across the lake to my house and we'd walk up the mountain. I wasn't too worried about it. Surely, it wasn't too bad.

We got on the plane and we were the only women on board. The only other people on the plane were a group of people who looked like they were from another country. They had matching shirts and seemed to me like maybe they were some kind of relief team. Maybe it was a bigger deal than I'd let myself admit . . .

We got off the plane and I started looking for a taxi. The airport was deserted, but there was one taxi in the lot that was taking several people to an area nearby. They told us we could come along, but when I told them where I lived, they told me they couldn't bring me there. The whole city was flooded. What? I just couldn't compute. I told him that my husband and my children were on the other side of the lake. I told him about my young daughter. He said, "Okay, Sister, we will try."

First, the taxi driver dropped off the other passengers. One man in his twenties was dropped off at the end of a street that soon turned to water. He headed in that direction, but we didn't wait to see what happened. I started wondering if he was going to wade home. As we drove to drop the others off, I could tell they were talking about us, asking the driver questions. I didn't understand their conversation because it was in a language that I don't speak, but some of the words were similar enough that I could tell that the passengers were asking, "Why did you pick up these foreigners? What purpose do they have being here during this crisis?" Then, my heart warmed as I heard our driver defend me. "No, you don't understand. She's one of us. Her baby girl is across the lake."

After he dropped them off, he turned to me. "Okay, Sister, what should we do?" I told him I wanted to try to get to the water. Maybe I could find a boat that would take my friend and I across. He said, "Okay, we'll try." We drove to a bridge area that was flooded out. We started to walk down to the water. So many other cars were parked there, people getting out, walking the same direction we were walking. Others were walking back, so we stopped to ask them. The answers were all the same. There was no way around the lake. There were no boats. All the boats were being used to rescue people.

At this point, I knew there was no point in continuing to try to get there that day. I figured that we'd just have to try to find a place to sleep for the night and hope the water had receded by morning. I asked our driver if he knew of a hotel. He told me, "Okay, we'll try." He tried to drive us to a hotel, but it, too, was underwater. We started making our way back toward the airport. He offered to have us stay in his house for the night. He told me, "My Mother would be happy to have you stay with her." I couldn't tell this very generous young man that my friend had a bit of the stomach flu and staying with locals was probably about the last thing she needed right then.

About that time, we saw a marriage hall. He pulled in. There were masses of people around the lawn and being dropped off by the truckload. People who had just been rescued from their homes. There were tables with relief supplies in the front. Our driver got out and spoke with the owners of the marriage hall. Then he came to me. It will cost you a bit, but there is a room here that you can stay in. I was willing to pay. There was no other option. I needed a private place for Gabriella to rest. We followed the owner up a few flights of stairs past families camped out in the hallways and large rooms on blankets. He opened a door and let us into a room. It hadn't been cleaned. There was still a chicken bone from someone's lunch and a few cigarette butts in the ash tray. At this point, Gabriella and I didn't care. We said thank you and closed the door on the swarm of people huddled outside.

Gabriella rested while I thought. We needed some food. We needed some information. We needed some way of getting word to Bill that we were on the other side of the city. Now, our phones didn't work. There was no electricity in the whole city. The restaurants were shut down. Shops were running out of food. What were we supposed to do? We ended up going downstairs to the relief tables and asking the nurses there what supplies they needed most. We had some cash that we could use. We saved enough for what we thought would bring us back to the Big City and took the rest to a supermarket across the street. We bought a few snacks for ourselves to eat, some bottled water and then baby formula and baby food for the relief tables.

As we brought all the supplies back, Gabriella told me she needed to go lie down. I couldn't blame her. But, as we walked up the stairs, I looked into the eyes of some of the women right near us. I let her go to rest and I started to talk with these ladies. They had all been rescued that day from their homes that were several stories underwater. They had all lost most of their things. They were all worried about their menfolk who had stayed behind to guard their houses from possible looting. Some of the homes were falling because of cheap construction methods. Were their homes still upright? Were their fathers, brothers, and sons alive? How long would it be before the water went down and they could hear from them?

In the middle of these stories, we were called downstairs to the big marriage hall. We were seated in groups of 4. Some of the women called me to their group. A large plate of rice with some vegetables and lentils was placed in front of us and we shared the meal, eating with our hands from the same plate. They laughed and told me that when the flood was over, I would be invited to their weddings where we could eat food together like this on a happier occasion. Several of the young girls were supposed to be married that fall. Now, that wasn't a possibility. They would have to wait until another year. They fought back tears.

One mother told me how her papers for moving to another country for work had been lost in the flood. She had plans to make a better life for herself and her son. But now, she didn't have another plan. Story after story filled my ears and filled my heart. As

I wondered about my own husband and children on the other side of the lake, my heart broke for these women. I knew that my kids and husband were fine. Our house was on high ground — very high ground. Our home was full of food — enough food for a month. My husband was the best planner and survival expert I knew. If he had to, he could take the kids up into the mountains and be just fine. I didn't need to worry about them. I just missed them. My heart ached for these new sisters. I asked if I could sing a song over them. I tried to translate it the best I could. I sang the song my Mother always sang to us at bedtime. A version of the Lord's Prayer. As I sang, the women's eyes filled with tears. Afterwards, I told them I was going to check on my sick friend. They thanked me and grabbed my hands, "Before you came tonight, we didn't have any hope. Now we have some hope. Thank You."

I gave them nothing except my prayer for them. I gave them nothing except my ear and my hand, my heart and my smile. This gift of hope was all from God. God gave them, and me, hope that we would be reunited with our families.

3

There was a time when I yelled at an army officer. It was during the flood. I was separated from my family. I couldn't call them. I couldn't get to them. I was heading back to the Big City with my friend, Gabriella, because there was no where for us to stay there and no way to get money. We had just used every spare bit of our money to pay for the baby formula and food the night before. We arrived at the airport only to find that what we had saved for tickets was only enough for one ticket. The price had doubled since there were so many people trying to get out of the valley. We had American dollars, but no one was willing to part with their currency since the ATMs were all closed. We were sitting around, waiting and wondering what we had to do.

Being a foreign woman, I had grown somewhat accustomed to the stares by pretty much everyone around me. It was obvious that my friend and I were different, but I'd been different for about two years now. There were boys on motorcycles that would pass a rickshaw I was on, slow down, and repass it. There were men who would stare at me as I walked by. There were groups of young men who would break into song as I walked past. There were people who stared out of curiosity and then there were the ones who stared inappropriately. It was pretty easy to tell the difference. On most days, I'd ignore them. Sometimes, if I was feeling spunky, I'd stare back until they became uncomfortable and looked away. Sometimes I'd say something, politely or rudely, as my mood struck me.

Well, my mood wasn't so great as I sat waiting with Gabriella. A man behind one of the counters had told us to just wait for a bit and he would try to find a way to change our dollars so we could take a flight that day. We were sitting and talking through plans, where to stay, what to do, how to pay for it, when I noticed that one of the army men, toting a machine gun, standing with his comrades, was staring at me very pointedly. I tried to just look away and ignore him, hoping he'd get bored and move along. He continued to stare. I changed seats so there was a pillar between him and me. He shifted his spot and continued to stare.

I had had it. I was scared, tired, stressed out, missing my family, trying to take care of my friend, and worried for my community. I cracked. I yelled across the room, "If my husband looked at your sister the way you are looking at me right now, there would be trouble!" His eyes got big. I'd yelled it in his language.

Everyone around us could understand what I'd said. His buddies could understand what I said. I glared at him.

His comrades started to laugh and make fun of him. "Oh, Sister sure told you! She's right! Haha! You just got told off by a foreigner!" Oh, it felt good. If I had been a local girl in a not-so-public place, I would never have been able to do that. I would have gotten into quite a bit of trouble. But, I was a foreign woman who was leaving that day. I was sick and tired of being scared of the men in this place. I'd said my piece and he sheepishly walked away. Whew!

A few minutes later, we were at the counter asking for help getting tickets. No one could change our money. About this time, an Italian army officer got in line behind us. I just had to try, "Excuse me, would you happen to have some rupees you would change for dollars?" Yes! he did! He was on his way home and could exchange dollars or rupees easily. We were able to get the cash we needed and buy the tickets. God gave me a safe trip to the hotel in Delhi after I'd told off a man with a machine gun.

4

There was a day we let our kids fly in a helicopter without us. I was back in the Big City. Bill and the kids were still in Lake City. We had very spotty phones and texting services. I had heard his voice a few times, but it lasted for five minutes or less and then it would cut out. That was the end of our conversation. There were some other friends who were in the same city as I was — trying to connect with friends or family members in the mountains. We were all trying to figure out what was best for everyone involved. It seemed like it might be some time before the roads were passable — it had already been seven or eight days. Supplies were starting to run low in the area. Power wasn't available yet. Bill was trying to spend his days finding ways to help rescue people from their homes or bring supplies where they were needed. The kids spent their days with family friends. There was no way of knowing how much harder things would get before they got better.

About this time, we heard of a way for Bill to send the kids with some trusted friends to meet me in the Big City so he would be more free to help there. My heart soared. It had been ten days since I saw my children — by far the longest time I'd ever been away from them or Bill. I started to pray. Bill started to plan. They would be driven to meet an army truck which would take them to a helicopter which would take them to an airplane which would take them to me. Bill helped the kids onto the truck, tucked in with the women in the front. This truck could navigate the flooded and muddy streets better than our cars could. Later, when we talked with our friends, they seemed to feel that this army truck trip had been kind of traumatic — people pushing to pack in and get the ride to the helicopter. We asked Carl about it — worried that the kids might have felt the same way. "How was the truck ride, Buddy?"

"Well, my leg was kinda smushed over like that. I was sitting on a tire."

"Was it better or worse than the Metro?"

"About the same."

We stopped worrying that the army truck had scarred him for life. Then, they were on a helicopter, across the flooded city, to meet the airplane. The only thing we could get from the kids was that it was loud and they had been told to keep their ears covered. They also found great joy in tattling to me which of the children on the helicopter hadn't obeyed. They seemed to think it quite normal that they would ride a helicopter to the airport. After this event, for at least a year, when we would tell them that we were going somewhere in an airplane, Josie would pipe up, "And a helicopter?" No, Jo, not every kid gets a helicopter ride to the airport before they're two.

Finally, after long waits and lots of negotiating, the weary group boarded the plane and I got word that they were on their way to me. I rushed from my hotel room. I could hardly stand it. I ended up getting to the airport well ahead of them and sat there in the heat for what seemed an eternity. Every time I saw a group of people leaving the airport, I would scan the crowd. Finally, I saw a group of people I knew from Lake City. "Mommy!!!" Carl yelled out and ran to wrap his arms as tightly as he could around me. I picked him up and carried him over to get Josie. Our friend had been wearing her in my sling — she looked as comfortable as could be but reached for me. I strapped her on and went over to the baggage cart where James was sitting. He was half-asleep after his ordeal and just stared at my face, "Mama . . ?" "I'm here, Buddy, I'm here!"

I wrapped them up, hugged each of our precious friends who had delivered to me my most precious gifts, and hopped in a taxi to go settle in to the hotel room. Gabriella met us and helped me tuck the kids in before heading off to her own room. That night, I slept with all of my kids around me. Bill was even able to call me and hear that they had arrived safely. I knew he was free to try to help our neighbors and I was free to be Mama again. God gave our family strength and safety.

5

There was a day I got my home back. While I was in the Big City with the kids, Bill was trying to help the people in Lake City. He was boating out to some areas to bring clean water or food. He was sharing some of our stock-piled food with neighbors who had not planned ahead so well. He was trying to make plans so that the business could help with the restoration efforts after the flood waters receded.

And then he got a phone call. Our landlord needed his house. Our landlord lived in the heart of the city and the entire first floor of his house was flooded. He and his wife were elderly. They couldn't clean and fix the house themselves. They were currently staying with a family member, but that family member had to fix her house as well. He told Bill that he would like us to move to another house in the area owned by his relative. We would pay the same rent for a bigger property and bigger home. But, we'd need to leave Amy and her family. There was another caretaker family already living on the property. Amy could still come and work for me, but we would miss their day in, day out presence. Bill hung up the phone and started packing. He was supposed to travel to meet us in two short days. He had only a day and a half to move our entire house to a new one — in the middle of a natural disaster — with no notice and no help from me.

Thankfully, our local friends came through again. They basically shoved all our belongings into several truckloads and hauled them to the new house, threw them in as best they could, and went back for more. With Bill and our friends working all day, everything was out of the house and it was clean before Bill got on the plane to come to me.

In the Big City, we cried together. We had loved our other house. We had been through such a struggle in these weeks already. The move had been especially hard on Bill, having to go through all the emotion and work without me. The reality of losing our home was especially hard on the kids and me. I was so thrilled to have Amy as part of my life and we hadn't even gotten to say goodbye to our house.

When we arrived in our new home, I immediately felt lost. All our belongings were in dilapidated piles on the floor of whatever room Bill thought we might want them. I started trying to make sense of this new place. I went to meet the new neighbors. I could immediately tell that this relationship was going to be different. This couple started trying to work angles from the moment we met. She wanted to work for me, but I told her that Amy was already my helper. They tried to get money for the gardening, but we already had a gardener. Several times, we found things missing in our home. Simple, silly, or small things like the kids' glow bracelets or candy or the keys to our outside door locks. We had to change the locks on our home four times. We couldn't trust this family in our house. I struggled to trust their children to play with ours, though I could tell that they were hurting for love and attention.

The hardest moment for me was on the day of Carl's birthday. We had a party with many families invited. We invited these neighbors, too. They left the party a little early, and as other children started to go, they couldn't find their bags of candy that Carl had given them as thank you gifts. Carl's was missing, too. I couldn't prove it, but I was pretty sure that these kids had taken them. I didn't want to accuse them in front of Carl, but he understood and was hurt that these children who he had invited had treated him this way. It broke my heart that my son had to learn about these things at such a young age.

Then there was a day when the wife was taken very ill. She had partial paralysis. I offered to take her to the doctor. As I waited there with her relatives, the doctor looked at me and asked, "Why did she ingest poison?" I was shocked. I had no idea that this woman was hurting so much that she was trying to end her life. On my encouragement, she went back to her home village with her parents for over a month. Her children stayed in the house. Her husband worked odd jobs and was away for a week at a time. Relatives came in and out, but often teenagers were taking care of each other in the house next door. I had no idea where I could turn to try to help them. I was struggling to manage my own house of young kids in a strange place. How could I raise these children, too?

There was no DCFS to call, no school to report to, and as far as I could see, no other person who cared. Finally, after weeks and weeks, the mother came back home. She seemed much better and her parents visited much more frequently. Also, she took the kids with her to the village anytime they had school breaks. I prayed and prayed for that family, but have no guarantee that anything has changed for them. I tried to talk to her about the hope I have. I even prayed for her healing. She seemed grateful but weary. I didn't have the right words to really reach her. I know that only God can do that.

After a year and a half of this wrestling and conflict, our landlord called. His home in the city was finished. Would we like to move back in to our old house? Yes!!! I had cried so many tears over that loss: the loss of my friend, the loss of my yard, even the loss of the crazy cricket players behind the house. I was sure that this was just one more thing that God was asking me to give up. Well, God did take my home from me. But God gave it back again. God gave me my home and a greater appreciation for the true gift that it is.

6

There was a day I drove on the left side of the road. Our family had lived in South Asia for over two years. We owned several two-wheeled vehicles in that time. Bill had become quite the motorcyclist. I, however, am the world's worst when it comes to balance. I fall regularly on a bicycle, so I didn't trust myself at all on a scooter. We moved to the mountains and our family realized that we really needed a car. Traffic moved faster there, our family was growing so that we fit much less comfortably than before, and it snowed. So, we started looking into getting a car.

I remember telling Bill that I'd never drive in this part of the world. When we arrived, I was sure that I'd never be able to navigate the cacophony of vehicles, pedestrians, and animals that plied the roads. There were very few stoplights. There were no stop signs. As far as I could tell, each intersection was a strange mixture between a wager and a compromise. The biggest vehicle could bet they'd have the right of way, but a pedestrian may just put out his/her hand as if to say, "I'm coming," and move right into the flow of traffic. Horns were used more a way of communicating than complaining. "Beep! I'm entering a blind turn!" "Beep! I'm coming up behind you, stay in your lane!" "Beep! Get out of the way, dog/goat/cow/human!" "Beep! Everyone else is beeping, so I'm joining in!"

Then there were things that mean something completely different than they did in my driver's ed courses at school. Flashing lights, which used to mean a broken down car or dense fog, now meant "I'm coming right at you in your lane. Move over." A turn signal, which used to indicate that a car was turning in that direction, now meant "you can pass me on this side." I started to realize that the multiple choice possibilities that had always seemed so pointless and obviously wrong at the DMV were probably put there because in some other country, they were actually the rules!

Because of my resolve, it only took about two and a half years for me to venture onto the road. It really was the isolation that drove me to it. When Bill was at work, I would have very little opportunity to get out. I would have to wait until he was home to drive our small family around. He was usually so exhausted from having to be out and about all week that he just wanted to rest at home. I decided I'd just have to conquer my fears and grab the wheel.

We found a small, used van that would comfortably hold our family. Bill planned a few easy trips to get me started: a trip to the garden nearby, groceries early in the morning, a friend's house not too far away. I started to feel more and more confident with what he called "Matrix Driving." As the driver, I needed to look ahead and anticipate what all the other drivers were going to do on the road ahead of us. This one was about to turn out from the side road. That one was about to make a U-turn. The one over there was going to stop abruptly to pick up a passenger. I began to drive more aggressively. I stopped using my rear-view mirror. I learned that it was my job to look ahead — always ahead. I needed to keep the nose of my car in play at all times. Sometimes one inch was all that another car needed to wiggle into my lane.

As I gained confidence, I drove further and further into the city. I would take another lady with me so that I could focus on the road and not my children. I would maneuver through traffic and over potholes, around herds of sheep and in and out of checkpoints. Later, I could even pack the kids into the car and go across town by myself.

I even drove to the village. Some women had come on a visit and it just made sense for us to go to the village alone. I loaded them into the car and we drove out of the city, down the winding, country roads, through several villages, backtracked after several wrong turns, but we eventually made it to the village. My local friends were shocked and thankful that we'd made the trip without the help of a man. I was thankful, too. Now, I know that I can visit my friends even when Bill can't. God gave me the courage and confidence to get into the driver's seat.

7

There was a day my son shared a hospital bed. That morning, we sure didn't think there would be a hospital involved at all. For a few days, Carl had been complaining that his ankle hurt. Well, that's pretty normal for an active kid. I asked him if he'd twisted it or banged it on something, but he didn't recall anything. Still, not too strange. Then, he started getting a fever. I couldn't see anything else wrong with him — no sore throat, cough, aches and pains — just a fever and a sore leg. So, after a few days, we decided to take him to the pediatrician in town.

We wound through the streets, in and out of the traffic, stopped at the little office above a restaurant, and went in. There were about thirty other parents there with their children. We'd gotten an appointment ahead of time and knew that we'd be seen in just a few minutes. They sat us down on a bench where several others were waiting. After each person went in, we moved down on the bench. People whispered, wondering who we were, but no one asked me outright, so I just focused my attention on my son. We chatted about small things while I periodically felt his head and wondered what the possible explanation could be.

When our turn came, we walked into the office and shut the door firmly behind us so that no one else could peek in to ask the doctor questions while we were being seen. He put Carl on the table, checked his ears, nose, and throat, asked about his symptoms, and told me that he had a throat infection. I told him about Carl's leg pain, but he said not to worry about that at all. He said that children often get bumps and sprains and it should be fine in a few days. I took the prescription for an antibiotic and thanked him. We went home.

I filled the prescription for Carl and gave him the first dose. Later, that afternoon, he was crying to me that his leg hurt so badly. I didn't really know what to do, but called a friend who had recently visited an orthopedic doctor in the area. She suggested that we take Carl to him to get an X-ray done. He just so happened to have office hours in our market that evening. So, at 5:00 PM, I took Carl down to the market square. At that point, he was limping into the doctor's office. The doctor put Carl up on the table, asked about his fever, pulled up both pant legs and felt the ankles with his hands.

He looked at me and said, "I don't want to scare you, but you need to take him to the hospital right away. They will do an X-ray there to be sure, but I am almost positive that he has an infection in his bone. If it is bad enough, he will need surgery right away. This cannot wait." I was shocked. I had never heard of a bone infection. He told me that they are rare in other parts of the world, but here, they can be quite common. He told me where the bone and joint hospital was in town. Carl and I turned out of the office and headed to the car. I wanted to carry him. My boy, just seven years old. I wanted to protect him from this, but I couldn't. We needed to get to the hospital.

I called Bill on my way home and we then called our friends. They agreed that our two small kids could stay over with his wife and that he, and two other friends, would come along with us to the hospital. We packed some food, some clean blankets, some clean water, soap, toothpaste, and a change of clothes. We had no way of knowing how long we would need to be there or what the condition of the hospital was. Our friend knew. He had been there before.

We rushed to the hospital. One person parked the car while the rest of us headed through the doors. It turned out that it was a very good thing to have so many people along with us. One person would wait in one line while another would wait in another line. We needed a treatment slip. We needed an X-ray. We needed to pay for these services. We needed to find the surgeon's office. We needed to get blood tests done.

The blood draw was probably the most traumatic for Carl. He has never liked needles. He screams and fights every time. They put him on a bed with another injured boy. He tried to fight off the nurses who came to take blood. They brought him to a small room where three people held him down so they could draw his blood. Then, we had to get an X-ray. In the room, I told them that Carl needed a lead vest put on him. They didn't have one. We prayed as they gave Carl the X-ray. These technicians did probably hundreds of X-rays every day and had no protection. I prayed for them, too.

After the X-rays were ready, we met with the surgeon. He told us that Carl's infection was large enough that a surgery was immediately necessary. We asked if we could wait a few days and he told us that was a bad idea. We must get it out as quickly as possible. He was very patient to answer all our questions. He was even willing to do a culture of the infection, though that wasn't normal practice. He reassured us to look up everything on google to make sure that what he was saying was accurate. I smiled at this. This professional — whose word was law in this culture — was willing to sit and answer our questions. I was humbled by him and encouraged that he was doing the very best he could for our son.

Then, we were brought into another room with about five beds in it. Carl had eaten a small dinner, so we had to wait until he had fasted long enough to be put under for the surgery. Carl was put on the foot of a bed where an old woman and her grandson were resting. I sat next to him and tried to read him a book we'd brought along to entertain him. He fell asleep for a bit and it warmed my heart to see him resting in the middle of the chaos. A young man on another bed nearby asked us if we'd eaten or if we needed anything. He asked what had happened to Carl and seemed truly concerned for him. His long beard and prayer cap would maybe raise eyebrows in other parts of the world, but here, in this unfamiliar hospital, he was the one who told us, "If you need anything, let us know. This is our place and we will help you." I found myself so thankful for that young man.

We looked at the clock and realized that Carl had fasted long enough. No one was coming to bring us to the surgery room. We soon decided that we must need to go and find the surgeon. So, we sent someone from our party to investigate. In our area, it's good to roll up to a hospital with an entourage. The larger your entourage, the more quickly you can make things happen. We were so thankful for ours so that we could focus on Carl. Soon, they were bringing us upstairs for the surgery.

I was holding Carl and then an orderly came in and took him from my hands. I watched as Carl was carried through the doors into the surgery room. Bill was handed a prescription for the things that were needed. He had to walk out of the hospital and down the street to get things like surgical gloves and anesthetic for the surgery. As soon as he got back, we sat together and prayed while Carl was in the other room. It probably took less than ten minutes. We were told that he was on a bed in the hall and that we could come to him. He was staring up at the ceiling, "There's a lot of lines up there." He wasn't quite all there. "Mama, you have four eyes." Oh, how I hugged him and laughed! I also almost fainted. I realized that during that whole ordeal I had had nothing to eat or drink. We quickly drank something and I ate an apple. Then, my knees would carry me again and we brought Carl back down to the main room.

They placed Carl on a bed where another boy was already sleeping. He slept at the foot. Bill found a stool and I sat on it, holding Carl's hand, Bill standing behind me. Soon, he encouraged me to lay a wool blanket on the floor and try to get some sleep.

There were other women doing the same. The floor was filthy, but I had no other choice. I lay down and closed my eyes. Bill took my place on the stool holding Carl's hand. Carl slept soundly and before we could fully sleep, Bill was interrupted by a young orderly.

They had cleared out a storage closet for us and put a bed in there for Carl. I took out the sheets we had brought along that we hadn't been able to use yet because he hadn't had a bed of his own since we started this horrible evening. Then, we laid Carl on top of them and I curled up next to him. Bill took my spot on the blanket on the floor near us. God gave us our boy. And he gave us a few hours' sleep.

8

There was a day I caused my son pain. We woke in the hospital the next morning. Carl was hungry, so we pulled out the packets of crackers and cookies we'd brought with us. Someone brought us chai. We Skyped our family in the States. It was wonderful to see Carl smile. People kept coming into and out of our room, but for the most part, we were alone. We waited for the surgeon to come and tell us what was next. When he did arrive, he seemed to bring every single doctor and intern that was working in the hospital with him. They looked at Carl's paperwork, his X-rays, and discussed the best treatment. We were told that Carl would need eight days of intravenous antibiotics and then probably about six more weeks of oral antibiotics. His wound had been left open so that it could heal from the inside out, thereby lessening the chance that any infection could be trapped.

We realized that these things would have to happen either in the hospital or at home. Since our home was so much less chaotic and so much more clean than the hospital, we decided to bring him back with us that day. They left an IV port in his hand so that injections could be given. We went home via the local pharmacy where the pharmacist agreed to visit us every day to administer the injections and clean the wound.

We put Carl's mattress on the floor in our front room so that he would have easy access to the whole family. He wasn't to put pressure on his foot for 8 weeks. That first evening, when the pharmacist came, Bill and I were there with Carl. We watched with pain as the pharmacist just pulled off the bandage on Carl's leg. It was stuck and hurt Carl pretty badly. Then, we had to hold him down as he cleaned it and then gave the injection into the IV port. The injections burned since they weren't diluted with saline like at most hospitals. After that experience, Bill and I talked and decided that we could do these things for Carl without the pharmacist — and maybe with more tenderness and patience. So, we told the pharmacist thank you very much for teaching us what needed to be done and we would do it from then on. We purchased all the medicine, bandages, etc., got some additional instructions from a doctor friend of ours, and started treating our child by ourselves.

I don't think anything can prepare you for holding down your own son while he screams, "Not now, Mama! Just wait! Do we have to do this? Please, stop!" Carl was such a strong, brave boy, but he didn't want to have to go through this pain. He didn't want to feel that, see that, experience that. Bill handled the cleaning of the wound. Each day, twice a day, we changed bandages, he rinsed out the wound with a peroxide solution, and we rewrapped the wound again. I did a load of laundry every day just trying to keep clean bandages and towels available for this process. For the first few days, I couldn't even look at the wound. It was just too deep and raw. It hurt my heart too much. But, after the first few days, it started to close and it looked clean. I could tell that it was going to be better.

Bill, however, couldn't handle the needles. He has a serious aversion to anything to do with veins. So, I was in charge of putting the five injections a day into Carl's hand. These burned him so badly and he fought us every time. It was so hard for us. One day, while we were holding him down as he screamed, I felt God say to me, "This is what I do for you, Maggie. You don't see that the pain you are going through is cleaning you, is helping you, is important. I have to let you experience this pain so you can be cleaned. But, I don't leave you alone. I'm right here, holding you." That night I wrote a song. "How far down will you find my sin? Has it been there long, can you tell me when? Will it hurt too much to clean it away? Do we really have to do this today?"

God was with us during this period in our lives as we watched our son suffer. As we even directly caused some of his suffering to bring about his healing. It was one of the hardest things that God ever asked us to do. Still, who was better to do it than the two of us who loved him more than anyone else? By God's grace, he does this with each of us, his children. God cleaned Carl's leg and brought full healing to our boy. God gave us a deeper faith and a deeper understanding of his patient, relentless, challenging, and complete love.

9

There was a day when I made blackberry pancakes. Lake City had become a difficult place to live . . . again. There was political and social unrest that made it unsafe for our family to venture out of our neighborhood. Stores were closed all day. Cars weren't supposed to travel the roads. No public transport was available. Angry protests filled the streets. Clashes between unarmed protesters with rocks and tear gas and pellet-gun toting forces were common. We could sometimes hear the chanting from our balcony or the popping noise of pellet guns or the deep booms of tear gas shells. We stayed inside our gate.

Thankfully, the unrest never reached up the hill where we lived. We were in a more isolated, less crowded area of the city, so as long as we remained at home, there was no real threat for us. So, for several months, the kids and I never left the hill. Bill would go into town on his motorcycle if we needed supplies. There were a few produce sellers and markets that would open in the early morning hours, so he'd return by 8:00 AM with whatever we'd run out of before the protests ramped up for the day.

We had friends on the hill. We could walk over to their houses for a visit or meet somewhere to pray and sing together. We would share meals and tea together. We would do our homeschool lessons, play a game outside, play a game inside, read some books together. We found things to keep us busy. But, it still got pretty draining. Imagine never going more than four blocks from your house for an entire month. Imagine straining your ears to decide if the yelling was from the boys playing cricket or the boys chanting on the road. Imagine trying to decide if the bangs you just heard were from someone building a new shed next door or from someone trying to disperse an angry crowd from your market square. It was so normal for us that we sometimes forgot just how stressful it really was.

Thankfully, just up the hill from our house, there was a mountain. On that mountain, the blackberries were ripe. So, we decided one morning that we'd start out early, bring our bucket, and collect blackberries. The kids were excited for the adventure — to get out of the gate and up the hill, into the trees and climbing on the rocks. We only had to walk up about three blocks of houses before we emerged onto a winding, stony path, through apple orchards, straight up the mountain. After about twenty minutes of hiking, Josie and James started to tire, but we reminded them of the ripe berries that awaited us, grabbed their hands, and half-dragged them along behind us. We'd stop every once in a while to take a drink and rest our lungs. We would sit on a rock and look out over the valley of our city. It was quiet up there. It was easy to imagine that the struggle and pain and isolation of the last few weeks was far, far away. We could let loose for a bit and just enjoy this exercise and fresh air.

Finally, after about an hour of hiking, we started seeing a few scraggly bushes peeking through the stone walls of the orchards. We stripped them of their ripe berries and moved on energized by our find and with the tempting taste of the tart berries on our lips. Then, we rounded a bend and saw the mother-load! Whole clumps of bushes with ripe berries hanging from them. We picked and picked. The thorns scratched our skin and pulled our clothes. We tripped over rocks, climbed over walls, and filled our bucket as quickly as possible. We sometimes had a hard time convincing the kids to put more berries in the bucket than they put in their mouths, but finally, we'd collected what we thought was enough.

Bringing the full bucket carefully back down the mountain, we took turns carrying Josie on our shoulders, since the rocks she had scrambled up on the way to the top were even more difficult to scramble down on the way to the bottom. When we reached our gate, we took off our shoes and I made my way to the kitchen. I found all the ingredients and the kids helped me mix the most celebratory batch of pancakes I think we'd ever eaten. Frying them on our pan on our stove, we could smell the sizzling juice of the berries. Our mouths watered. I made a fresh batch of "maple" syrup with brown sugar, water, and artificial maple and vanilla flavoring. I piled the pancakes on the plates, spread them with butter, poured out the syrup, and we sat down at our mat on the floor. Ah, an amazing treat! God gave us blackberry pancakes when we couldn't even go and buy toilet paper.

10

There was a day I claimed my homeland. Our rented house in the mountains looks over an empty plot. It is a large, terraced, piece of land that used to be apple orchards. But when the owners fled the violence decades ago, the land lay fallow. Now, it is most often used as a cricket field for the local boys and young men. On any given Sunday, we can have around 300 cricketers from ages ten to thirty-five. There will be three to four games going at once. The bottom level is reserved for the most serious games and in the upper level, where the playing field is rougher, the youngest players will organize their own games. On school days, the numbers are smaller, but there are still games played on that lot almost every day.

I was excited to think that these cricket matches would be played right outside my house and that my kids could watch them. It kind of turned the other way around, though. All the curious local boys would stand at my fence and watch my kids and I in our garden. It was very frustrating in the beginning, but after the novelty wore off, they were less likely to come. Also, if some struck up conversations, I would walk down and join in — trying to help translate. This made most of the young men nervous, so they would eventually walk away.

We had a trampoline that friends had given us, one of those big ones, without a net. Our kids loved that thing. We had set it up when we lived in a different house and then moved it with us to the new place. Trouble was, all those boys could see our trampoline from their cricket field. I often looked out my window to see a boy sneaking across our garden to jump on the trampoline. They were usually to big for it and often broke the springs. Soon, it was unusable. If I would go out and confront them, they would quickly jump off, pretend as if they weren't jumping, and say that they were looking for their ball that flew over our fence. Balls were always flying over our fence. We ended up just taking the trampoline down.

Another challenge was our water. We had two outdoor pumps and boys would yell at me from the cricket field, "Auntie, Auntie!!" When I would finally give in to their calling, they would ask me to give them some water from my pump. Now, this wouldn't be a hard or bad thing, but there were 300 kids out there. They interrupted me several times a day. I was getting frustrated. I started telling them that I wouldn't give it and that they'd have to bring it from home. After I started refusing, I got fewer requests and they found their water somewhere else. I noticed they never asked any of my neighbors for water . . .

One young man was particularly persistent, though. He was in charge of getting the cricket pitch ready for the serious matches. He wanted buckets of water to sprinkle on the pitch. He would come every morning with this request.

He came with several friends and asked for water one day. I told him no. It simply wasn't possible for me to come every morning and give him water. I had to give my own children breakfast and teach them their schoolwork. He would have to bring water from somewhere else. He looked me in the eye, something that in this culture was either very familiar or very confrontational. He was confronting me. "We belong to this land. This is our water."

I looked squarely back at him, "Who is your father?"

"Why do you want to know?"

"I want to tell him how rudely you are speaking to me."

Immediately, his posture shifted and his attitude changed. "No, no, I just am asking for the water. Our cricket league keeps kids off the streets, stops them from doing drugs and pelting stones."

"Why don't you ask one of my neighbors for water, then. It is someone else's turn to help you."

"They will not help me. They are not like you."

I was having a hard time following him. First he tells me this is not my land or my water and then he tells me that I am more generous than the people who belong to the land. I didn't have time to give him a lesson in logic. So, I repeated, "I don't have time to be always coming to give water."

One of his companions piped up, "Where are you from?" This is a common question. I can speak the language, though not well, and I may dress the part, but I will never be seen as a local. Still, I had my chance.

"I am from here. My husband works here. We rent this house here. My landlord calls me his American Daughter. We were here during the flood. We were here during the strikes and protests. This is my home. God made all of us and it is His world, not ours. I am His daughter and you are his sons. This is all of our home." I had tears in my eyes. My voice cracked. I had spoken the truth. It was the first time that I had truly claimed this land as my own, but I meant it. Even if I didn't belong to this culture, I belonged in it. Even if I wasn't born in this land, it was born into me. The young men all looked first surprised, then thoughtful. Each of them started nodding and agreeing with me. "Yes, this is your land, too."

After more conversation, we finally came to an agreement. I would give them water for two more weeks and that would give them time to work out another arrangement. They also promised to keep young men and boys from climbing into my yard. The persistent young man even started calling me 'Auntie' and invited me to have tea with his mother some day. Since that conversation, we have had very little trouble with the cricketers. They play their games and we play ours. Sometimes, they still come to chat with my kids. About once a week, I still get a group of boys who want some water. I still tell them to bring some from home. God gave us some peace and honor in our community.

11

There was a day our money stopped working. We were getting ready to go to the Big City to see our friend, Ethan, get married. He had been our friend and Bill's language helper when we lived in Kite City. We were so excited to share in this day with him. We paid for the plane tickets, booked a cheap room, and started packing. It was two days before we were supposed to leave the country and our money stopped working. All over the country, the paper money was no longer valid. People were waiting in three hour lines to get the equivalent of $35 of new bills from the ATMs. People were waiting in five hour lines at banks to trade their void bills for new ones. People who had never had a credit or debit card before were trying to apply for one and learn to use it. It was complete chaos and we were going to the Big City.

Ethan called us telling us that we really didn't have to come. He'd understand if we didn't make it. But, how could we do that to a friend who had been there for us so many times? So, we collected up a few small bills that were still valid (about $40 worth), grabbed our coin jars, and got on the flight. I had planned to purchase appropriate wedding clothes when we reached the city. We had planned to eat at the hotel where we were staying. We thought we could just take cheap autos everywhere we wanted to go. But, when we arrived, we had to use prepaid taxis because we could pay with our card. We found out that our hotel didn't have a card reader, so we couldn't pay for the hotel itself, let alone food there. Thankfully, Bill had brought along some American dollars. The hotel would take these in payment.

We figured out that if we ate breakfast on the street, we could do so for around $1. We drank cups of chai and ate flatbread with potato and onion, dipped in lentils, on rickety stools pulled up to a folding table, next to the public urinals. These urinals had no doors around them. Several men used them while we enjoyed our breakfast. Our kids still talk about how delicious those flatbreads were, though, so I guess they were worth the dollar.

I took a trip to an area where I could use my debit card and found an outfit I thought would work for a wedding party. I made my way back to our hotel and we all got dressed up and headed to Ethan's family home where everyone was gathering for the wedding. The actual wedding was in another small city about a two hour drive from his house. We were to travel with some family friends, so we didn't want to be late. We found out quickly that we needn't have worried. I walked into the house and started to sigh relief as I saw that Ethan's sister-in-law's outfit was a similar style to mine . . . until she apologized that she hadn't gotten ready for the wedding yet. I settled for the fact that I was going to be the out-of-touch Westerner again.

We relaxed with some relatives as everyone started getting ready for the wedding. Ethan came into the room to chat with us as his mother brought us some tea and snacks. He started to tell us how nervous he was. "I shouldn't be nervous, though," he told us. I corrected him. "Of course you should be nervous! Your fiancé is nervous today. She is leaving her home and her family to be with you. You should be nervous that you will be a husband who deserves her sacrifice."

"Yes, Sister, you are right. I want to be a good husband." I could spend the rest of the evening hopeful that this couple would have a loving, committed relationship.

Finally, the wedding party was ready to get into the cars and we drove to the venue. It was a beautiful lawn decorated with lights and fabric. A platform was in the front where the groom would sit. The bride was still getting ready in an adjacent room. There were buffet tables with all sorts of foods for the guests: spicy noodles, sweet and tangy sauces, fried rice with meat, syrupy desserts. Ethan has several brothers and one of them, we devised, had been assigned to make sure that we enjoyed ourselves. He promptly sat our family down at a table and proceeded to order various cousins to bring us plates of food and cups of "coffee." The coffee reminded me of gas-station cappuccino.

We started meeting some relatives, but then the requests for selfies began. Our "Bodyguard Brother," as we started calling him, started to apologize for the rudeness of the other guests for making us feel uncomfortable. We assured him and assured him that this was our normal life, but he continued to chase people away and apologize.

After about an hour, it was time for Ethan to make his entrance. We walked over to get a better view of him walking in. He was wearing traditional wedding dress and was being escorted by his sister-in-law. All his relatives were pressed in around him. The mood was celebratory and majestic. All of a sudden, Bodyguard Brother came to my side. "Your brother wants you to come. Hurry, you must come." I took the kids' hands and Bill followed as I was escorted up to Ethan's parade. I sheepishly came in behind him and followed with the rest of the family. Later,

"Bodyguard Brother" explained that the sister of the groom escorts him to meet his bride's family. Since he had no biological sister, he had wanted me to escort him. I was stunned. Ethan had been through a lot with our family. I had taken a lot of liberty, scolding him, challenging him, and basically acting as only a big sister would. Still, I was utterly humbled at this gesture.

Later in the evening, I was brought to meet his lovely fiancé. She was very sweet but soft-spoken as a bride must be. I told her how happy I was for her and that if my brother did not treat her well, she should come to me. She smiled. Her mother surprised me still further by asking me to sit at their family table. I talked with her about my life as a farmer's daughter, about my family, about my faith. She did the same. She told me again and again how thankful she was that I was so "modest and simple." I guess the fact that I couldn't afford any fancier wedding clothes paid off!

Bill enjoyed a position of honor as well, sitting next to Ethan on the platform with the rest of his family. The kids ran all over the wedding hall, drinking all kinds of coffee brought to them by doting Aunties and Uncles. Time passed this way until the bride and groom were ushered into the waiting car. Tears were shed as the bride hugged her family. Hugs were passed around and then, at the early hour of 1 AM, we piled into the other cars and made our way back to the city. God gave us the chance to bless our family in that place.

Some Final Thoughts

God gave. Did you notice that? In every situation God gave what was needed. Resilience doesn't start with us. It starts with Him. Each time we find the perseverance to stay, to move, to go, to try, it is given to us from Him. We don't have this power within us. It is His gift. Just like faith. Just like hope, trust, joy, courage, love. It is a patient, relentless, pressing presence in our lives. When days and moments are difficult, even impossible, God gives what is needed for that day and that moment.

Our culture revolves around what is instant these days. We live our lives looking for the next thing to post on Instagram. We want instant gratification. We even cook our meals in the Instant Pot. But, God is forever. He is not rushed. He moves for the long-term — the really, really long-term. In His plan, things don't happen immediately. Even Jesus was born a baby. What a waste of thirty good years!! But God, in His incredible wisdom, uses the process to bring about His plans.

If I cared about my immediate happiness, about seeing immediate results, about measuring my immediate success, I would have packed my bags long ago. If God cared about those things, He would have helped me pack. But I can trust that His purposes are beyond what I can even see or know.

I can point to no concrete victory in these five years unless it is the victory of staying. Lake City is now my home. I have family there. I am family there. This is the work that God has done in me. I have no guarantee that there will be more to it than that. Hopefully, in another five years, I can write a new book, maybe called "God's Fruitful Girl" . . . ? But I'm not promised that. If I'm still where He's placed me and things are still hard, I can write a different book: "Still Stubborn." If I never see 'fruit', if I never 'make a difference' in others' eyes, if I never understand why He has me there, it is still enough. It is enough to know I'm called. It is enough to know He is faithful and is making me faithful. It is enough to be God's Stubborn Girl.